Patty is probably one of the most instrumental to listen and hear, her knowledge and experie] makes her one powerful writer, strategist and] anyone out there writing about partnerships, it should be her. Patty Soffer is the Steve Jobs of Partnerships; she makes us think different!

—Johanna C. Salazar, Founder
Aceneth Integrated Media

What I love about this book is that it's not all left-brain as most books on business are. It has heart, it's spiritual, and it's about relationships and the energy between people in business. You have accomplished something amazing.

—Birdee Golden, Department of Pathology
University of California San Diego Medical Center

Patty Soffer is boldly ushering in a new paradigm in business. She is a vibrant force of clarity, creativity and brilliance. It's impossible to be in her presence without coming away with a fresh perspective. With her distinctive personality—funny, sharp and clever—she tells it like it is. ALWAYS.

—April Norris, Instructor, Coach,
Healer and Creator at april-norris.com

I couldn't be more excited that Patty has packaged her wisdom, dramatic stories and special sauce into this book. Having waited for years for the release, I'm breath-taken by her impenetrable commitment to making partnerships successful. Her words are potent, as is the invitation to take inventory no matter where your partnerships stand today.

—Jessica Kizorek, Founder
badassbusinesswomen.org

"Partnership or Partnersh*t: You Decide" is evolutionary for modern business relationships. Patty's intuitive approach to defining and guiding the delicate nuances that affect our business lives goes way beyond mundane philosophy and strategy and into something very personal and exciting. She boldly shoots straight to the heart of what affects every relationship: It's not about financials, bricks and mortar, or technological advances, but about PEOPLE. Patty's book is like an experienced best friend guiding your hand from the formation of a new partnership to a successful, well-run business.

—Jose Luis Martinez, Creative Director
Miami World Cinema Center

If you are looking into forming a partnership (personal or professional) or creating something bigger for your life, this is whom you will want as your coach. Not only is Patty Soffer a creative soul, poignant public speaker, advocate for the arts and intelligent thought leader, but she is also a heart-based connector. She's done the "tough" work—using her own life as the litmus test. From that place, she helps people and businesses create a more "human" foundation in their personal and professional enclaves.

—Joe Lombardo, Partner
ETC Creative, New York/Chicago

I can't remember a text in law school that had so many practical applications. Soffer walks you through her P2P Process with stories of real partners destroying their business, and shows you how the process could have either saved the business or prevented the partnership from happening in the first place. While this book is a hands-on evaluative workbook for prospective partnerships, I daresay marriages could also be saved using Soffer's practical magic.

—Karen Hensley, Esq.
Hensley & Associates, Buffalo, NY

In our The Human Foundation seminar, my partner and I were shown the tools that we needed to make not only our business relationship better, but also our personal relationship. We learned that as much as we wanted to keep our business and personal worlds separate, we couldn't. For us, business is personal. Because we have now developed our Human Foundation, we have been able to learn how to communicate with each other. We are now prospering in both worlds. Thank you Patty Soffer for this amazing experience.

—David S. Greenwood, Owner
Danny Cardozo & Co., LLC

The Human Foundation's P2P Process exposed the exact difficulties we have been experiencing. Seeing things in black and white allowed us to view our situation from a rational perspective and point us in the direction of a solution.

—Susan Miner, MA
President, Beauty From the Inside Out

Also by Patty Soffer

Mom Said:
Moments and Memories of Life with our Mother
with Kathy Berger

The World According to CF

PARTNERSHIP
OR
PARTNERSH*T:
YOU DECIDE

HOW TO BUILD YOUR BUSINESS PARTNERSHIP ON
THE STRONGEST FOUNDATION THERE IS:
A HUMAN FOUNDATION™

BY
PATTY SOFFER
WITH VICTORIA ST. GEORGE

A HUMAN FOUNDATION PUBLISHING, LLC

This book may be purchased for educational, business or sales promotional use. For information, please contact A Human Foundation Publishing, 3716 NE 208 Terrace, Aventura, FL 33180.

info@ahumanfoundation.com

Partnership or Partnersh*t: You Decide. How to Build Your Business Partnership on the Strongest Foundation There Is: A Human Foundation™. ©2012 by Patty Soffer. All rights reserved. Published in the United States by A Human Foundation Publishing, LLC

http://www.ahumanfoundation.com
http://www.partnersht.com

Cover design by Danny Cardozo, DC&CO, dannycardozo.com

Author photograph by Danny Cardozo, DC&CO, dannycardozo.com

Interior design, composition by Vanessa Flores, sobe-creative.com

Library of Congress Control Number: 2012915193

ISBN: 978-0-9859173-0-2 (Paperback)
ISBN: 978-0-9859173-1-9 (Electronic Publication)
ISBN: 978-0-9859173-2-6 (Hardcover)

Printed in the United States of America

*I dedicate this book to all who are
partnership-bound or bound by partnership.*

It's rough out there.

*Be a safe harbor for yourself and one another, cherish what you have,
and do absolutely everything you can to protect your partnership.*

It takes consciousness, compassion and clarity.

WHAT I HAVE LEARNED IS THIS:

BUSINESS
IS
PERSONAL

CONTENTS

You are personally responsible for everything that happens in your life once you realize you are personally responsible for everything that happens in your life.

—Bruce Lipton, Ph.D.

FOREWORD

BY George I. Rosenthal

We are indeed fortunate in our lives when a confluence of seemingly serendipitous events come together to create a memorable experience forever etched in the far reaches of one's brain. Such was the case when I first met Patty, on a crisp fall evening in New York back in 1978. I was visiting a friend at his townhouse when into my sight-line came a vision, descending the stairway, who simply took my breath away. She was so naturally beautiful, had a wonderful radiating smile and a self-assurance that was clearly evident. Hello Patty!

As I got to know her, it also became evident that Patty was the most endearing and empathetic young woman I had ever met. Not only was she a great listener, but she also contributed a focused and considered response to my questions.

As the evening drew to a close, I found myself falling in serious like with Patty—and so began a friendship that has spanned decades. For me, the definition of a true and lasting friendship is one in which you never feel left behind in the growth of that relationship, and can always return to the warmth of your past experiences irrespective of intervening events. Although there have been significant gaps between our get-togethers, we have always been able to pick up where we left off without skipping a beat.

Over the years, I had gained clarity and insight that as able and adroit as Patty has always been in reaching out and taking care of others by providing support and understanding of their needs, there was a missing piece necessary to balance the equation: she did not take care of her own needs at that same level. She has paid a big price and has finally said, "No more."

While I believe most of us will acknowledge that it is so much easier to recognize the error of the ways in others rather than ourselves, Patty took a look into that mirror and did not like what she saw. Her journey has taken her to a place where she now clearly understands that relationships must serve the needs of both. She has personally felt the pain she speaks of, and has stepped forward to do something about it. Her disappointments and failures have been dissected, analyzed and reflected upon. Out of the crucible of her failed partnership and financial disaster comes a woman transformed, who has discovered through insights gained from listening, research, self-analysis and never giving up, the foundational requisites for sound, fulfilling and productive associations and interactions.

Partnership or Partnersh*t: You Decide asks the questions we should all be asking if we are to be successful in any of our relationships. The book helps you find your way to honest and thoughtful answers by identifying critical areas that must be mastered so you can build your own strong, human foundation, upon which can be constructed long-lasting partnerships in what ever form they may take, be it business, marriage or just plain high-quality friendships.

This book will provide readers with the knowledge and insights for how to best take care of themselves, while understanding what is required for our counterparts to feel supported and cared for as well. Without the balanced understanding of each others' hopes, fears, wishes and needs, it is not really possible to keep the teeter-totter of relationships in proper balance. And when that balance is lost, someone is going to come down hard.

I urge you to read and ponder the wisdom. You will come away richer for the experience.

George I. Rosenthal
Chairman
Raleigh Enterprises
Santa Monica, CA

ACKNOWLEDGMENTS

Writing a book is like having a baby—you can't do it alone. This process, which has taken me from crushing loss and pain to the germination of an idea to the fulfillment of that idea, has been brought forth because of some incredible, loyal and inspiring people.

To start, I have to go back to the real beginning, which means Mom and Dad. To say a mere thank you to these two incredible people is like winning a million-dollar lottery and then sharing only a penny. There are not enough words that can convey how deliciously inspiring, supportive and loving they have been in my life. Dad, I miss you every day, but I get all your messages from the universe. Keep 'em coming! Mom, while dementia may have stolen your mobility and cognition, your smile radiates and your loving heart beats strong. I feel you all the time. Too bad the world missed out on experiencing your wide array of super-talents: drawing, writing (especially your funny, quasi-porn poems), cooking, gardening, hostess-ing, mom-ing and playing concert piano having never taken a lesson, all the while selling Avon to pay the bills for a happy family of eight in a small Midwestern town. No one in my life has touched me like you do. I am who I am because of you. I bow down.

Now, to my kids . . . Adult children are a breed apart, and have much to teach—about listening, letting go, being accountable, trusting that their paths have been selected especially for them and trusting that all will be well. Sammy and Alex, I admire your bravery and drive and always have you in my heart. To say that I love you just isn't enough. I am proud, amazed and humbled by both of you. I sit in the bleachers of your lives and cheer you on each and every day. Go kids!

Friends make my world go 'round, and I have been blessed with a funny, crazy, accomplished, spontaneous, lively, silly, smart, loyal, world-traveling tribe who I love beyond all reason. Karen Hensley, Kathy Berger, Phyllis Apple, Carole Pumpian, Debbie Cheroff, Rhonda Fine, Dotty Barrie, Jane and John Sutton, Stuart Geller, Mark Bender, Ellen Gould, April Norris, Osmara Vindel, Danny Cardozo, David Greenwood and Vanessa Flores, you have been there, stayed close, helped me grow, made me laugh, put up with me and held me to the light in the darkest of times. Whether it's circumstances or miles that separate us, we are never apart in our hearts. Love you lots.

Next, to my teams at Soffer Adkins and The Soffer Collec+ive:

We made some serious magic together, and that only happens once in a lifetime. The connection we had, the love we shared, and the laughter, tears, highs, lows, wins and losses, were all treasures, and I miss each and every one of you every day. While our end came suddenly and painfully, it makes me happy to know that you have all gone on to other great things and are sharing your immense talents with an appreciative world. There was no better time in my life than when we were together. You are the genesis of this book, and I thank you for being wildly, passionately and authentically human. I keep you in my heart and want you to know that not only were you great teachers for me, but you set the bar for how a business culture should be.

Finally, to the amazing Vicki St. George, who stepped out of her comfort zone so I could step into mine: Vicki, your generosity and humanity are why I was able to develop and complete this project to its absolute best expression of service. You prodded me like a goat heading up the mountain, and wouldn't even let me pause long enough to pee in the bushes. I thank you so much, and can now decree that from here on in, the word "ass-ume" and its unique spelling, belongs to you and only you. I believe it should have its own dictionary definition, or at the very least, a mention in Wikipedia. You truly rock.

INTRODUCTION

If you want good answers, ask good questions.
—Tony Robbins

My sister Kathy asked me this not long ago, during an evening of reminiscing and reflection:

"If you could go back to any time in your life and redo it," she said, "What would that be?"

It was a good question; I instantly knew the answer.

"Without a doubt," I said, "I would go back to when my partner and I started our business."

That it was my sister asking the question was particularly poignant since she was one of our original five team members. She had been there from the beginning, and was as deeply attached to our blended business family as I was. Those were joyful days for all of us—a culmination of sorts for me, and the happiest and most fulfilled I have ever felt in my life.

"What would you have done differently?" she asked next, not realizing what buttons she was pushing. (She knew I was writing a book but had no idea as to its contents.) The answer to that came fast, too, but my journey to the place where I *could* answer with clarity and conviction did not.

"I would have done everything I could have to protect all that I loved," I said, feeling sadness about what should have been. "I would have built a Human Foundation."

For nearly a decade, our amazing branding + design company led the market in our region with innovation, creativity and passion. We were innocent and free, loved what we did and loved each other beyond words. Our company was the kind of place where you could write on the walls, hand-make a book, experiment with infant technology and somehow make it work, promise more than you could deliver and then deliver more than you promised. We encouraged wild abandon and broke all the design biz rules, mostly because we didn't know them. That's how creativity is set loose, unbridled, and our company reeked of it, along with spunk and sheer fearlessness. I had a soul relationship with the company and everyone in it, with all that it entailed. So you can understand that when it failed, the pain literally brought me, sobbing, to my knees.

Just like that, this gem of a company and all that it stood for was gone.

I spent the next three years in a fog, traveling, attending seminars, learning, writing, thinking, meditating and talking to people to try to find exactly what went wrong. While some people just shrug, pay the lawyers and walk away, I *had* to know. How did this happen? This was some journey, but I emerged wiser, more compassionate, self-aware and mind-blowingly clear as to the culprit.

Huh?

Who, me? What do you mean, me?

What did I do?

It was all *his* fault!

Ahhh, nope. It was not.

Ok, that was hard to digest. But it was the very piece of the puzzle upon which all further growth would depend.

As much as I wanted to blame someone else for everything that went wrong, what I have learned is this:

It's not about the other person. It's about *you*, your self-awareness, what you create for your life, what you allow into your life and how you manage it.

But he . . .

No—not he, she *or* it.

You.

Oh crap.

+ + + + + + +

To get to be this aware, I had to start over, give up all pretense and question everything I believed in. There were times I fought it like a rabid dog and other times when I just wanted to say, "Screw it. Who cares anyway?" Well, I cared. And you should too, because awareness will change your partnerships, relationships and your life. It did mine.

Becoming aware took every minute of those three years, filled with pain with no analgesic relief, intense soul-searching, countless dollars, air miles and hotel rooms, more trust than I had ever had, more humility than

I would have believed possible and more tears than I thought a body could produce. I wanted answers and was not going to stop until I found them.

The answers were not fast in coming, but when they finally came to me, they arrived in the form of questions—really good, beautiful, human, open, enlightening, honest, challenging yet simple questions. So good, so pure, so basic I was stunned.

That's it? Could it be that simple?

These were things that I of course had thought about—don't we all?—but had never point-blank asked myself or my partner, nor he me. We weren't idiots; far from it. With every good intention, we operated on autopilot, typical for partnerships (and for most people). We assumed we knew each other, and ourselves, but we were just not operating on a conscious level. We were too successful, giddy, happy and busy to be conscious. Anyway, who had time? We were too busy to talk. Too busy to ask. Too busy to listen. Busybusybusybusy.

I'll tell you this: Being too busy might one day result in your not being busy at all. Because you could busy yourself out of everything—like I did.

WHAT I HAVE LEARNED IS THIS:

> **A HIGH PERCENTAGE OF BUSINESS PARTNERSHIPS LAUNCH WITHOUT THE PARTNERS HAVING ANY REAL, DEFINABLE SELF-AWARENESS.**

I wrote this book to share some of the answers I discovered in my search for self-awareness, in business and otherwise. However, my answers won't be your answers. In fact, your answers won't be found in this or any book. They can only be found inside yourself. This is a "how" book to help you discover the answers unique to you and your business. It will give you the really good, important questions that will show you how to get to know yourself and your partner, what you want, what works for you and how you can work together.

I have turned these questions into a seven-step process to help you build your partnership the right way. I call it the Partnersh*t-to-Par+ner-ship Process because that is exactly what it is. Let's not mince words here: This process will clear away all of the sh*t that, left to its own devices, will eventually sink your -ship. How? By opening your consciousness to accept that people, *starting with you*, are the foundation for absolutely everything that goes on in this world, and that *you are accountable for absolutely everything you do.*

Whoa. I can already imagine the look on your face as you read this. "Maybe you," you're saying, "but not me. It's all because of that loser partner of mine." Well, if you're saying things like this, either you have lost a partner or business or are losing one. You're feeling the pain. You are pissed. I know because I constantly see it in my clients' faces (and saw it in mine). We all want to blame someone else.

Sure, your partner might be a heinous slime ball; he or she might have lied, cheated, run a Ponzi scheme, disrespected your mother or slept with your mate. Maybe he was a bully. Maybe she stole. Or maybe he/she was adorable, nice, funny and helpful but just not partner material. Whatever. It's irrelevant. We're not here to talk about that beyond this one simple-yet-obvious question:

Who let this person into your life?

Again, you.

You chose them. So if they're pissing you off or not pulling their share, it's not their fault. It's your fault. They're in your life because you drew them to you—and you are allowing them to remain.

If you've reached this point, it's not because you're evil or stupid. It's because you are not conscious. Face it: You cannot control another person. You can only control yourself and what you are thinking and doing. And if you are thinking your Aunt Millie will be a great partner once you finally get her to stop drinking or that your current partnership cesspool will somehow miraculously clean itself up, I'm going to have to reiterate: you are not conscious.

Yeah, this was not exactly the sweetest tasting humble pie I ever had to eat either. It took me a while to get past my ego and to realize the truth, but the thing about being conscious is this: once you're conscious, you're conscious. There's no going back.

Bringing this powerful fact to your attention has become my life's work. Business (actually, everything) must be about you becoming aware of *you* first; then the partner(s), and then the business. You must be 100 percent aware and accountable for what goes on in your life. You might think you already know this on some semantic level, but I will bet you've not thought *consciously* about it. It's time we all do.

Not being self-aware is deadly. Not being accountable is deadly. So, too, is taking others for granted. You have to start with you and build from there. You create this foundation by being human first; by getting to know yourself. Then and only then can you approach the people you want to partner with, ask—and answer—the *right* questions, and *listen* to their answers with an open mind and an open heart. Once you're aware of who you are, you'll know immediately whether that other person will mesh with you and whether this is someone whom you will welcome, allow even, into your life as a partner. And understand that once you do, it is incumbent upon you to cherish and nurture this partnership and do all you can to make it work. Should you choose to take a pass, congratulate yourself for being so aware and walk away with grace and dignity on both sides.

To get respect, you must give it. To get love, clarity, compassion, dignity, contribution and gratitude, you must give it. Start by eliminating the constipating business attitudes and faces that people put on for each other. It's all a façade, and façades are impossible to maintain. Be who you are! Declare it. Stand by

it. You and you alone will determine the energy in your partnerships. Again: *It's not about the other person.* You owe it to yourself and everyone around you to be the best expression of yourself—who you really are and not some robot looking for approval. Don't betray yourself by saying yes when you mean no. Don't look for kudos. Look for the authentic you. Only then are you ready to be a partner.

Figuring all this out was an intense process. I'm big on process, which is what one would expect from someone with my background in brand strategy. Process gives things order and helps them make sense. Writing this book was a process. Through it, people would ask, "Why is your book taking so long? So-and-so wrote hers in 60 days." Well, I had much to learn, so time was part of my process.

Also, any process takes patience, so I had to learn to be more patient. Ultimately, that my process took three years is irrelevant. Things take as long as they take—I mean, it took me nearly a decade to screw this all up. So what's three years? That it healed me and now enables me to now help others is the only thing that matters.

Realizing that mine was 100 percent a partnership failure and not a business failure changed my understanding of how critical healthy partnerships are to a business.

Realizing that my partnership failure ultimately had *nothing to do with my partner* changed my life. This was a pretty big aha moment, and it blew holes in all that I had believed and held dear. I not only had to change my beliefs but my thoughts and behaviors. It was a life-shift of massive proportions.

The truth is, most entrepreneurial newbies do not have a clue about how to run a business in the first place. We know what we know—how to design a garden, practice law, treat patients, paint houses, give massages, build houses, do sheet-metal work and so on. How many of us have any idea how to actually run the *business* of doing all those things? Probably very few, if any. Add two or more unaware, unaccountable partners to that mix, and you have three strikes against you before you even start. These are not good odds for success.

Par+nership is not for everyone. Neither is business. And the statistics are sobering: more than one-third of partnerships will fail within the first two years, while 55% of new businesses will fail within the first five years.[1] So proceed with caution. For those of you who want a great, healthy partnership and a shot at having a successful business, I wholeheartedly believe you need to do this process before you build your business. However, if you're already on your way, it will also work for businesses in a growth stage or for partners who are stuck and/or are serious about getting their sh*t together before they blow everything.

And it's never over. You need to keep going back to the process for tuneups, just as you need to keep learning about and adjusting yourself every day. Change is a constant. You and your partnership are and will forever be a work in progress. Life ebbs and flows, and so will your partnership. Once in, *you must keep talking to one another and asking more and more good questions* so you don't end up where I did, buried in partnersh*t.

Ok, you might be asking, what exactly is a *good question*? That's a great

---

1   Small Business Administration

question! Thanks for asking.

A good question is one that starts with listening: You must listen to the other person's chatter, opinions, comments, word choice and body language to understand where they are coming from and what it is they're really asking. A good question is an honest attempt on your part to discover or unveil something that will be important to not just you but both of you. Good questions often evoke emotional responses so be careful not to interrogate. Ask, listen and don't judge. Then, dig deeper. Ask "Why?" relentlessly. Once they answer, ask why again and again. I promise, you will get to the bottom of things and to the real answer using this method.

Steve Leshansky, CEO of Optimize International and one of this nation's most highly regarded business coaches, advises keeping the focus on the person you are talking to, not on yourself, and using superlatives when asking questions. For example, asking "What is the biggest reason why you want to become my partner?" will get you a better, more focused answer than will "Why do you want to become my partner?".

Predictably, once I figured all this out, Monday-morning quarterbacking kicked in: Had I known then what I know now, perhaps our company would still be in existence; perhaps my partner and I never would have partnered in the first place; perhaps we would have had an exit strategy to minimize the pain; perhaps, perhaps, perhaps. . .

I'll never know. What I do know is what *wouldn't* have happened is what did.

The self, health, relationship, legal and financial toll when partnerships fail is devastating, with collateral damage strewn everywhere. You can avoid my mistakes for the cost

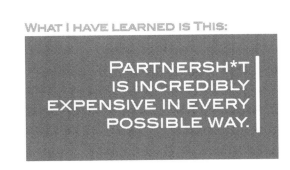

WHAT I HAVE LEARNED IS THIS:

PARTNERSH*T IS INCREDIBLY EXPENSIVE IN EVERY POSSIBLE WAY.

of this book. Seems like a pretty good deal to me.

PART ONE

HOUSTON, WE HAVE A PROBLEM

1

SH*T GOES ONLY ONE WAY, AND THAT'S DOWN

Knowing yourself is only difficult if you are afraid of your own magnificence.
—Danny Cardozo

Life started to really suck right around mid-2006.

Our branding and design company had just come off a great year. Soffer Adkins was well known in the Miami/Fort Lauderdale area and were fast becoming a national force. Our design superstars were creating winning brands and collateral campaigns for industries like hospitality, healthcare, real estate, entertainment, food and fashion. Our employee base was growing, we'd won dozens of industry awards and clients were coming at us like the ladies to George Clooney. On the surface, all looked good.

Except I was starting to feel unhappy. Something had changed. What was happening to me? What was happening to our cool little business? Yeah, things were cruising along, but something felt *off*. There were people everywhere—what were they all doing? *Be careful what you wish for...* Our phones blew up all day long. We were producing some of the best work in the entire Southeast and were in the viewfinder of some pretty cool potential global clients. We'd just been named one of *Entrepreneur Magazine's Hot 500 Businesses* in the nation; we were billing big money and landing big accounts.

And yet, one day, there it was—we had "success-ed" ourselves into operational chaos and debt not just up to but beyond our eyeballs.

Most upsetting was the growing tension between my partner and me. I had loved the guy like a brother since we met nearly a decade earlier. At the time, he was a 21-year-old junior art director at an agency I had used as a resource for my business plan/grant/request-for-proposal (RFP)-writing business. I was an ambitious in-my-40s single mom and recent college graduate looking to expand what I was doing into something more visually creative. He was sweet and kind and talented, dedicated and hard working, and an absolute wunderkind when it came to tech. We settled into a cast-of-*Friends* existence, working and socializing together, first in that agency and then in our respective small businesses, until one day we decided, "Ahhh, what the hell, let's just become partners."

And that, people, is how it usually happens. You grab a family member and open a dog grooming business. You and your college roommate see a bright future in landscaping over a few too many beers. That stylin' friend seems like a perfect let's-open-a-store partner for you because, hey, you're pretty stylin' yourself. You and your neighbor bake cookies for the school PTA sale and the next thing you know you're a budding Mrs. Fields + 1. You've all heard the legendary started-by-friends-in-a-garage stories about Apple and Microsoft. The birth of a partnership is rarely any more scientific than that, and not many stop to take a look at themselves first.

I know I didn't. I just happily blasted ahead without a care in the world, and I was no wide-eyed kid. My partner and I both loved design and branding. He was teaching me tech, and I was a voracious student. I was a writer. He was a designer. I had tons of connections. He could sit at his computer for countless hours and crank out one cool design after another. I'd sit beside him, soaking it in and loving it. He was calm, patient, and insanely optimistic and made me laugh. I was fiery, equally optimistic, high energy and made things happen. We both wanted our own agency so badly we would do *anything* to achieve it. How could we go wrong? I thought we were the perfect blend of different. Like long legs and Louboutins, we were good on our own, but oh so much better together.

We shared a dream, the most powerful thing people can do. But like so many others, we forgot to clearly define it. Instead, we launched that dream on hope, excitement, serendipity, fearlessness, faith and trust—and incredible naïveté. Honestly, without all this, nobody would ever go into business. I mean, would you *willingly* sign up for stress, problems, fiscal exposure, legal risk, infighting and 70-hour workweeks?

This was not my first business—more like my fifth—but it was my first partnership. I knew the business would absolutely kill. I felt it in my gut. What I had yet to learn is that we would unwittingly kill *it*.

We jumped right into the middle of all this, which, of course, we thought was the beginning. It sure *felt* like the beginning, based on other businesses I had owned. I know now that this is typical, predictable behavior for a new, wet-under-the-collar partner-biz. Most (perhaps all?) partner-businesses inadvertently start in the middle: they name the biz, create the logo, do the website /brochure/business card tango, buy the equipment, rent space and go to work, with little regard for what the partners want individually or together. Let me tell you: the road out of that hellish middle, when it comes (and it will) is ex-pen-sive and pain-ful.

We opened with a small office and five people. We had neither plan nor strategy other than to merge his clients with mine. . . but we sure had plenty of passion, plus killer designer office furniture and whatever Apple had to sell (and this was pre-iAnything).

We got busy fast. Before long we were working for clients like FedEx,

Ritz-Carlton, Starwood, Marriott, the Humane Society, RCTV and more, with McDonald's, Related Group, MDM, Carlyle, Midtown Equities many other pedigrees waiting in the wings. We were a good team and made it rain like crazy. Soon, we were going too fast to slow down. We worked dog hard, loved what we did, laughed a lot, played a lot, and had talent, drive, reputation and an economic boom in our favor. Plus we were good people wanting to do good things. The perfect recipe, right?

For a while, it was. This approach actually worked for quite a few years, beating the 55-percent-of-new-businesses-fail-within-the-first-five-years odds. We'd thumbs-up each other all day long, not believing our good fortune and not even remotely conceiving that it could ever end.

Best of all, we had become deeply connected to each other and our employees, many of whom were family members—humble, supportive and optimistic. But in retrospect, it's clear I had no idea what my partner wanted in his heart. And though I can't say for sure, he probably had no clue what I wanted either. How could he? Even I didn't know. Because we were cruising along and things were rockin', it never occurred to either one of us to take the time to ask. I know it didn't to me.

Meanwhile, our original five employees had grown to 20, and then we were 40. We became the most popular agency in town because we were kicking out amazing work, had a great reputation with clients and were good to our people. The two-hour lunch breaks, office parties, dinners at great restaurants, beach picnics and end-of-day *Call of Duty* marathons didn't hurt. We were a family. A loyal, hard-working, deeply connected family. We were having a blast and it was absolutely freaking awesome. I felt strong and purposeful.

But our luck was running out, as luck does. I see now that my partner and I had not developed much beyond the original connection that drew us together in the first place. At least, not on any level that would ensure longevity. We were trying to do it all but, as it turns out, not much of it well, outside of our personal God-given talents, typical for entrepreneurs and the cause of immense frustration. We were also getting lazy about our partnership, perhaps taking it for granted. We started to drift into the "doing our own thing" trap.

Next came some dumb decisions. We had already moved into a bigger space once, but then we moved again, against all practical advice. Sure, it was 4000 square feet of terraced gorgeous-ness (important here in the Sun Belt), but we never analytically discussed the reasons for moving, beyond believing it would bring new business. The cost was ridiculous, with no clear payoff in sight. Also, we were diluting our roots and drifting into the advertising business, making the classic mistake of letting the marketplace define us. Our clients, many of whom were benefiting from the real estate boom of the mid-2000s, asked us to help them with their advertising, so understandably, we jumped in headfirst. One problem: we were a branding and design company and had no clue how to manage the hybrid ad agency business model that we had developed. We were taking clients that made no sense for us. Plus, as we quickly found out, bigger was not better. It was just bigger.

Most deadly of all, we had stopped communicating. The reality is this: You *must* have constant communication with your partner. Overcommunication is a requirement and the people in your life must understand and accept it. Initially we were probably overcommunicating. We were available to each other 24/7. But now we passed each other in the halls without saying much more than hello.

While these might sound like business problems, they are partnership problems first. Good, conscious, solid partners do not make decisions without deep digging and endless discussion. They communicate constantly. They set goals and then stay on the same page to further those goals. But like a dysfunctional marriage where both parties start looking for solace outside the relationship, we had begun to look outside our partnership for what we needed. We stopped looking inside and to each other, where all the answers should—and would—be found.

> NOBODY CAN BE ALLOWED TO INTRUDE IN YOUR PARTNERSHIP. YOU HAVE TO BE PERCEIVED AS A SOLITARY UNIT. THE MINUTE YOU OPEN PRIVATE CONVERSATIONS TO THE REST OF THE TEAM OR EVEN TO FAMILY MEMBERS, YOU WILL CREATE PARTNERSH*T.

Partnership success requires looking inward, following your heart and doing what you love. If you have no sense of self, you get lost and everyone suffers, which is exactly what happened. We both just rolled along, working so hard on all but the partnership, and things got more complicated by the day. We had started out playing "small design firm" and now we had 40 mouths (plus wives and kids) that all needed to be fed, clothed and insured. We ran with it, and ran and ran and ran, but neither of us knew exactly toward what we were running. There wasn't a strategy or even a goal, except to be "the best" and "big" and "awesome" and all manner of euphemistic banter. While this was great, positive energy, which every business needs, one has to ask: how does this translate into dollars?

> CHAOS IS COSTLY.

Answer: it doesn't. At least, not dollars that you get to keep.

Is this what we had dreamed of building? I

hoped not, because it was freaking me out.

I have always been blessed with beginner's luck: I killed my first pinball game and walked away with hundreds of dollars playing poker one night, the only time I ever played. I won contests, took major life-risks, fancied myself informed and worldly and always landed safely on my feet.

Landing on my ass was a whole different sensation.

IT STARTS WITH YOU

Okay, I admit it: I was the one who wanted to be "big," and I also admit I had no clear idea of what that actually meant (that and a million other things, as I was to discover). So how could we possibly define "big" as partners? "Big" cannot just be some nebulous blob. That's like saying you want to be "rich." Or "tall." Or live "out West." What does that mean to you?

A clear vision requires a) self-awareness first; b) accountability; c) clear definition of desired outcomes; and then d) management of the inevitable change that occurs daily. It has to start with what you want,

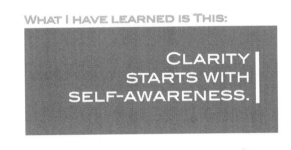

WHAT I HAVE LEARNED IS THIS:

CLARITY STARTS WITH SELF-AWARENESS.

then with what the partners want, and then how you together see the business fitting into your lives. You have to listen to yourself first. Trust yourself. Then talk to each other. It is imperative that you do not surrender your power through anger and frustration.

Because we had no clear vision and weren't talking, we started to drown. Truth be told, we also were in over our heads when it came to running a business of this size. A company with five employees is oh-so-different than one with forty. At heart, we were the creative and marketing talent of the firm, and neither of us had the skills (or the desire, at least not on my part) to be this new kind of leader. What we really needed was a rock-star CEO, but we didn't realize that then. Instead, our world started to crack. I actually had one seasoned star employee come into my office with tears in his eyes and ask me if he could please quit. Wow. That's a first. He could see what was happening, it clearly made him sad and probably disgusted, and I suppose he didn't want to be around for the inevitable Armageddon.

Worst of all were the cracks that were eating away at the friendship my partner and I had shared for so many years. Friends should be able to talk. Instead, this thing called "Our Partnership" was suddenly looming large, like a separate, green-eyed monster.

WHAT I HAVE LEARNED IS THIS:

DO NOT KID YOURSELF THAT FRIENDSHIP/ RELATIONSHIP/ PARTNERSHIP ARE ONE AND THE SAME. THEY ARE NOT.

Is there a line between the -ships? You bet there is—a razor-sharp barbed wire line. And it will cut you when crossed.

I realized this when *all* of our -ships turned to -sh*t.

Instead of us finding a workable solution together, instead of us just simply talking to each other, we started to fight.

ROLLING IN THE DEEP (SH*T)

Even though things weren't great, I never *ever* considered that my partner and I would ever fight, as in really *fight*. That's a lot of nevers and evers, but that's how foreign the concept was to me. That I was in a foreign country when the big explosion finally came is equally, well, *foreign*.

The Information Age, while totally progressive, gives us the tools to say things we'd never have the guts or stupidity to say in person. I was coming apart and had gone to Mexico with some friends to decompress at a spa week. Clearly I had missed the thinking behind "decompress." Instead, I spent most of every day in the hotel's computer room banging out accusation after accusation directed at my partner and receiving the same in e-plies. The breakup process had begun. By Thursday, all out war had been declared, and it wasn't between the U.S. and Mexico.

We had at it in a way I'd not experienced before, with the Internet serving as the conduit for the bashings. This had been brewing for a long time, and at a time when it was critical that we cut the crap and speak face-to-face, there we were, hiding behind a keyboard.

I despise email for what it cannot do. It's a lousy way to communicate anything more than nonemotional details like "please pick up the dry cleaning" or "your car will be ready at 2pm." I see people making this mistake all the time. I do it too. Beware. Email is an assault weapon; in the wrong hands it will cause a world of hurt. Our e-war created Grand Canyon-deep pain and I knew then it would be a long, probably impossible climb to extricate ourselves.

In retrospect, I see our demise was inevitable. Our partnership was like a wild child—endearing but without clarity, structure or healthy boundaries. We had gone from living in our hearts, as children naturally do, to operating from stubborn bull heads. There was no middle. Heart and anything remotely connected to it had been destroyed.

The "boundary" that we now erected was far from

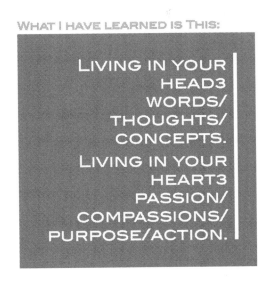

WHAT I HAVE LEARNED IS THIS:

LIVING IN YOUR HEAD3 WORDS/ THOUGHTS/ CONCEPTS. LIVING IN YOUR HEART3 PASSION/ COMPASSIONS/ PURPOSE/ACTION.

healthy; worse, it was made of cement—impenetrable and final. Here's what's real: Unless you have a strong, heart-based foundation for your partnership, you will create your own cement wall with your name on it.

I face-planted into mine.

WORK IT OUT OR GET OUT

We had opened our company five months before the September 11, 2001 tragedy and most of our clients were from the hospitality industry. Travel everywhere screeched to a halt, and we could have too. Instead, we looked at each other, said "real estate" and moved forward. Stupid luck? Yeah, maybe it was a little bit of beginner's luck at work again. More likely is that it was the two of us being totally focused and super-aligned, which is common at the beginning of any new venture. Those months after 9/11 could have been a huge challenge to our survival, but since we were still on our "honeymoon," we tended to agree about most things. We had a good, strong energy connection.

But that was then. Five years later our behavior had descended into something you'd expect to see in a schoolyard full of bullies. It only took two more years to permanently destroy everything. Sure, partners fight, as do spouses and friends. Fighting can be a good thing if the rules are established and the visions match, making it safe and clean. If not, it gets dirty. You get hit—and you hit—below the belt.

WHAT I HAVE LEARNED IS THIS:

> MOST PROBLEMS ARE LESS ABOUT CONFLICT AND MORE ABOUT BLAME AND JUDGEMENT.

Blame and judgment are two of life's most destructive forces. It would have been nice to set all that aside and instead, talk to each other about what was happening to us. But because we were not aware, we were just doing what we knew how to do. So it got dirty. We stopped acting like partners. Partnersh*t took over.

WHAT IS PARTNERSH*T?

Well, it's pretty much self-descriptive: Partnersh*t is that place you reach in your partnership where everything starts to go bad. It begins simply enough—a dig there, a jab here, that moment when you begin to disregard, ignore, or worse, placate your partner. Before you know it, you've got separate agendas and everyone and everything begins to suffer.

Here's what Partnersh*t looks like:

- You lose respect for each other.
- You pretend everything's cool.
- You stop talking to each other.
- You talk about each other behind backs.
- You create factions.
- You listen to outside advisors and not to each other.
- You lose focus.
- Your passion dies.
- You start making emotional, not business, decisions.
- Your business begins to suffer.
- Your creativity dips.
- You stop having fun.

Are you noticing all the "You's" here? This is not a passive event. Creating Partnersh*t takes a whole lot of energy, all of it negative.

WHAT CAUSES PARTNERSH*T?

Partnersh*t results from lack of mastery in five key areas:

1. Lack of self-awareness

2. Lack of accountability

3. Lack of clarity

4. Lack of defined outcome

5. Inability to manage change because there was no basis for re-negotiation (which stems from all of the above).

What does all this mean in plain English? It means there is:

- Negative energy!
- Lack of consciousness!
- Lack of defined values!
- Lack of defined goals!
- Taking each other for granted!
- Blame!
- Judgment!
- Not talking to each other!
- Not asking good questions!
- Not listening to each other!
- Ass-uming!
- Laziness!
- Anger!
- Lack of trust!
- Wishin'!
- Hopin'!
- Thinkin'!
- Prayin'!

It only takes one or two of these things to destroy your partnership. So if you're doing *any* of this stuff, you'd better act fast or you'll soon be too buried to dig out.

We were beyond buried and then some. I could not believe it. I mean, this person was my long-time friend—someone I loved and respected.

What the f#!% were we doing?

Our breakdown took time (breaking down is a process too, and does not happen overnight—think about trees as they turn golden in the fall, and then die a stark, brown, crunchy death), but we were so deeply into disintegration mode that there seemed no way to stop it.

Worst of all, our employees were bearing the brunt of it, analogous to kids suffering as their parents duke it out in a messy divorce. Here's what's true; maybe it will be enough to stop you in your tracks:

- Your employees want guidance.

- They want structure.

- They want rules.

- They want a strong foundation.

- They want you to feel secure, empowered, accountable, proud, so they can too.

Employees need these qualities in their leader; without them, they cannot be excellent nor can they have job security.

Our team was dying for us to get our sh*t together because if we blew up, so would they. They were seeing what we couldn't. They sat by, helpless, and watched with broken hearts as our "family"—blood and bonded—came apart.

Being fearless had always been my specialty, but suddenly I was terrified. What should have been just garden-variety business bumps turned into heavy turbulence because we had no foundation from which to fix things. Through it all, I knew in my heart that my partner was a good person. *I* was a good person. And *this should not be happening.*

To top it all off, personal-life things had changed for both of us, as things do: marriage, aging parents, shifting priorities and such. I see now that we did not give any of these events the respect and attention they

> LIFE'S EVENTS TAKE THEIR TOLL AND WILL ABSOLUTELY AFFECT A PARTNERSHIP. ANYTHING THAT AFFECTS A PERSON AFFECTS A PARTNERSHIP.

deserved. Fatal mistake.

With no roadmap or tools to help us adapt, we ultimately took aim at each other's wallets and hearts—classic reactive behavior to strike where it hurts the most. I admit it. I crumbled. I could not believe how hard this hit me. I mean, I was no pushover, and over time I had grown a massive set of chick-balls that had always served me well. Now they just shriveled, along with my ego, confidence and spirit. I was left with boxes of Kleenex to sop up the tears and crates of Advil for the constant headache. Some leader I was.

At one point early on in the disintegration process, we actually did reach out to a consultant to help us, but I didn't feel nurtured or safe with the person we chose. I also felt this consultant did not understand the core of our problem but rather proceeded automatically with what he knew how to do. I had no idea how my partner felt about the consultant because I didn't ask him.

Duh.

This light bulb moment hit me two years after the fact.

I had no idea how my partner felt. About anything. I still don't.

Why?

Because I never asked. Because I wasn't listening.

Not too much later, our partnership could no longer handle the strain, and we pulled the plug.

Partnersh*t took us down.

DEAD IS AS DEAD DOES.

I will never forget our final day. It was the same day they found actor Heath Ledger's body—what a metaphor that was. I felt dead too. The energy in our office was dead. People wandered around like after an explosion, not knowing what to say or do. There was no air. It was hard to breathe.

A partnership breakup destroys way more than the partnership. It destroys:

- Self-esteem
- Security
- Trust
- Identity
- Ego
- Health
- Friendships
- Spontaneity
- Happiness
- Sleep

You cry. You feel betrayed. You blame everyone. All you want to do is get under the covers and hide. But you can't because guess what? There's more! Yes, my friends, there is so much more. You still have responsibilities. The fragments of the business are still there, like a lingering hangover, needing triage-like attention and care. You still have employees. Between furtive whispers, they look at you in fear and disbelief. What to do with all this?

The joke is, without an exit strategy you don't even get to decide. The decision gets made for you.

We had both made a rookie partnership mistake: blindly signing for a bank loan as "Joint and Several" signatories without checking with an attorney, which means both of us together were liable for the debt and each of us was individually liable as well. That's common enough, right? Well, so is the common cold. That doesn't mean it's good.

If you Frisbee this book into the trash can right now, you've learned the one huge lesson that I beg you to never forget: <u>Money issues will destroy even the best partnerships.</u> So pay attention, ask good questions and please see an attorney to help you determine and master the legal partnership entity that will best serve you.

Financial differences rank high on the list of why business partnerships fail. And it's not just because one might spend more than the other. That's too simple. You need to dig deeper. *Financial philosophies and the reasons behind them* are critical to partnership success. Sure, sometimes out-and-out theft is the culprit, but most cases are like mine, where well intentioned but uninformed, naïve decisions lead to disaster.

Think about something: if your partner comes from a wheeler-dealer gambling mentality and is cool with it, that philosophy will touch every aspect of the partnership, including and especially, the financial area. Marry that with someone who comes from scarcity and is afraid to lose a dime and it isn't going to matter how well the two of you get along—the partnership will have a fundamental flaw. Neither perspective is right or wrong. They're just different, and the divide will be too great to overcome. You cannot beat what is ingrained. Don't even try. That is called trying to change someone and we already talked about how well that works.

You must be *intensely* self-aware about your financial philosophy and then *thoroughly and intensely* get to know about theirs. And just so you know, banks and creditors could care less about your broken partnership, broken heart, lost friend or depression. They *are* Willy Sutton: they, too, go where the money is.

In our case, that was to me. Because we did no planning, I "got" it all—the debt, lawsuits, sales tax judgments, bills, taxes, payroll, lease obligations. All of it.

A Pyrrhic victory.

Now what?

2

AND THEN THERE WAS ONE

Our feelings about ourselves are actually the most important barometer
for determining the condition of our lives.
—Anita Moorjani, *Dying to Be Me*

Like it or not, what was left of the business was now mine to sink or save. Not only did I not want it, but I also had no motivation to solve the critical issues I was now facing alone—because clearly, *I had no idea who I was or what I wanted.* If I did, I never would have allowed this to happen. There was no lonelier time in my life.

Because the company was in crisis, I was thrown into parts of the business I had no business being involved in. Me, in finance and operations? I might as well have tried to quarterback for the Miami Dolphins. I was overwhelmed with cleaning up a mess that looked like a New Orleans frat house after Mardi Gras. Those were some dark, dark days. But there were a few glimmers of light and a couple of colleagues who steered me back to what I was good at, helping me see the possibility of a new day.

Enter the rock-star Hockenstein girls. Valerie H., my controller, was

> FIRST RULE OF
> BUSINESS:
> SPEND 90% OF
> YOUR TIME DOING
> WHAT YOU DO BEST.
>
> SECOND RULE OF
> BUSINESS:
> HIRE A ROCK-STAR
> GENIUS TO DO
> WHAT YOU AREN'T
> QUALIFIED TO DO.

a definite rock star. She was a late entry into the old business and willing to stand by me in the new. Her warm heart, calm nature, patience, optimism, cheerleading and financial genius provided me with a trusted haven. She made sure I was aware of everything but untangled me from running the financial side of the business. Smart move. Valerie brought in her sister-in-law Tammy H., a New York-trained rock-star brand strategist, to help us get back on our feet. It was time to be quiet, listen, and let these people help me. God knows I needed it.

We were true cobbler's children, barefoot and wobbly. Tammy represented stability, knowledge, experience, process and strength—things I was unable to provide at that moment. The remaining team members loved her. There she was, teaching our disheveled, despondent but willing little group that we still had it and that we could become the company we were meant to be. Under Tammy, the Soffer Collec+ive was born.

Look at the + sign. It's not the first time you are seeing it in this book, and it's not a brand trick. I fought hard for the idea of a collec+ive because no matter what I had just gone through, I believed with all my heart that people are better together than they are alone. We are all part of a collec+ive on this planet, and what one does affects others. I didn't want this new company to be all about me. I was starting to learn some things about myself and knew that, more than ever, I hated working alone.

I wanted to be deeply connec+ed to the people I worked with. I wanted to learn how to be in a connected partnership and wanted my team to be as invested in our future as I was. I still believed in par+nership. I had just stopped believing in me.

We began to piece together a new foundation for our business—a foundation composed of the very elements that I had never addressed for myself and that my partner and I had never addressed. In our enthusiasm, we had never bothered to build any foundation. (Like most small partner-business owners, we simply didn't know any better. And we're not alone.)

Hmmmm, a foundation. A seed was planted . . .

Over the years, I had picked up book after book to help guide us, but most business books were either corporate drone-ons or clones of the "10-steps-to-starting-a-business" philosophy (know your product, know your market, know the competition, know how to price, know how to charge and so on). Nobody was talking about how important it was to *know yourself first, and then to know each other.* Those that did touch on people did so from a legal, consultant or corporate perspective—important, yes, but it didn't resonate with me. While I read a blame tome or two, nobody was sharing their personal stories of failure and redemption, and there was no mention of relationships or how critically important they are. Nobody had a solution. So it's no wonder we got lost. The business world was generally unconscious to this.

Now, with Tammy's help, our little army was coming back to life in a very human way, because we had all been in deep pain, a great motivator. People will do anything to get out of pain, including drink, smoke, take pills, eat or sleep. I chose learning as my drug. I was searching for the remedy, not the fix, because I was not ever going to do this again.

As a bonus, we were even having a little fun. It wasn't exactly a party, but it was a start.

We were talking. Listening. Going inside ourselves. Taking just a peek at what was in there. Arguing even, but in a productive, safe way. Who were we? What did we want? How would we work together? What did we want to be? Where did we want to go? Who did we want to serve? Who was in? What were we willing to do to get there? What did we want out of this business? What were we willing to put into it? Who was I?

Man, this was starting to look like a plan. I liked it. The order of things was making sense; it seemed process-y. I was alone, without an official partner, but I began to think of everyone on the team as my partner, and it felt good. I realized I wasn't totally burned after all. Crisis brings out the best in people and this scared, shell-shocked but loyal group stood up like soldiers. It was a beautiful thing to behold. We were creating something together from the rubble. Slowly, we began to rise again. By mid-2008, I thought that maybe—just maybe—we were out of the woods

Like before, I was inclined to move full speed ahead into this new enterprise. We repainted the office and created our new branding. Of course we did—old habits die hard. But thankfully, I was in enough pain to listen to the voice of caution that was holding me back. No, I declared, hands on hips, to anyone who would listen, I really was *not* going to do that again. But what was I going to do?

WHAT I HAVE LEARNED IS THIS:

> IF YOU ALWAYS DO WHAT YOU'VE ALWAYS DONE, YOU'LL ALWAYS GET WHAT YOU'VE ALWAYS GOTTEN.
> —TONY ROBBINS

I get now that I was talking to myself because I knew I could have easily repeated the same mistakes. People do it all the time. I was in new territory and that's when we tend to revert to our old ways because it's all we know. Just ask the woman whose husband beats her but who stays with him year after year.

I wasn't ready to bring on my own destruction with another ill-informed business partnership, so I understood I had to take a new road.

But how to start? Because I was still deeply entrenched in blame mode and had not yet reached the point where I would accept accountability for my part in the mess, I had no clarity around what to do next.

After much thought, many sleepless nights, and immense frustration, the fog started to lift and I came to some basic, human 101 realizations:

- Anything you do in life starts with you.

- What you want, feel, do, say and think creates your destination.

- You must be your own best partner first.

- A good partnership starts with a good you.

- All partnerships are about people.

- All partnership success comes from people.

- All partnership problems are people problems.

- People mess up because of lack of clarity about what they want.

- You must get to know yourself first to achieve clarity.

- You must get to know your partner on a deep level to achieve clarity.

- To do this, you have to ask the right questions.

But what were those questions?

SO I WAS THINKIN' EVERYTHING'S GONNA BE ALL RIGHT . . .

It had been nearly eight months since the breakup of my partnership, and I dared believe all would be well at the Soffer Collec+ive. We were working hard and digging out from our financial snowstorm. We had bitten the bullet, gutted our overhead and planned the move to smaller quarters. Still, we could feel a draggy-ness in the marketplace. Something was wrong. Now what?

In late September 2008, we found out the economy of the United States of American was on the verge of collapse. I did not see that coming. Truthfully, not many did. We had all drunk the "There's No Bubble" -flavored Kool-Aid. So there he was, Treasury Secretary Hank Paulsen (he of "the worst is likely behind us" and "it's a safe banking system...") looking dumbstruck as he delivered his statement before the Senate Banking Committee. As I watched, I remember thinking I hadn't cornered the market on fear. The guy looked like he was going to puke; I was right there with him.

The government bailout began. The markets tanked. Those "sound" banks collapsed. The real estate industry and those supported by it—our company's bread and butter—imploded. Hospitality and travel once again went bye-bye. Every day it seemed another competitor closed their doors. Clients disappeared. Many of my friends lost their homes. Their jobs. Their marriages. My investments were destroyed.

Really? I couldn't believe it. After everything that had already happened, now this?

WHAT I HAVE LEARNED IS THIS:

THE ONLY THING YOU CAN CONTROL IS YOUR THOUGHTS.

Henry Ford once said, "If you think you can or you think you can't, you're right." Well, Ford was right. In the end, it all came down to me and what was in my head. Billings were down, but we were still working and still had a good client or two. Yet try as I might, all I could think about was doom, gloom and failure. I had no emotional discipline left in me. Sure, the economy blew. That did not mean my business did. I was the one who decided it blew. It became my reality simply because that is what I focused on. Ask Valerie. She fought me on this and told me to stop thinking that way. She even told me to take a break and let her handle things for a while. I should have listened to her. But noooooooo. Instead, I gave failure all my energy. I was like the racecar driver whose constant thoughts of hitting the wall end up with—you guessed it—slamming into the wall. And just like that, it was over. Again.

But again, not done. There are no movie endings here; no fade-to-black for me. No such luck. Instead, it would take nearly every dime I had saved for over a decade (that's a whole 'lotta dimes) to clean up the mess. It would shatter every belief I ever had. It would call on me to surrender all that I knew for all that I could be. And then, it would gift me with the most amazing learnings of my life.

Clearly, this movie was just beginning.

3

THE WAY OUT IS THROUGH (NOTICE IT'S A PROCESS...)

Failure isn't fatal, but failure to change might be.
—John Wooden

"So this is what my house looks like," I said, as I wandered through it, with no other place to go. I had not been "home" in 10 years, so to speak. I had, by choice, worked day and night, and had lost sight of what was simple and peaceful. Those phones that used to be on fire were now silent. There were no clients calling because there were no clients. No office issues to solve. No team to take to dinner. No pride in a job well done. No kudos. No big checks. No teaching to do. There was nothing but quiet. Nothing but me and the cleanup, and no amount of Oprah, CNN, sitcom reruns or books would fill the void. I was just beginning to learn that only I could fill it, and only from the inside. Apparently a rebirth was in order.

I was down, but staying down just wasn't a long-term option. Rebirth is a messy process, what with all the wailing and resistance and anger and blame and fatigue and such. It's also a ton of hard work. You have to start by stopping what you're doing and just be. That's it. That's hard.

Think about that for a minute. We're so conditioned to *do* that we forget to take time to be. And that's why we're unconscious. We're always moving. We live in an achievement society and are measured by our output. "Rebirth School" gets you refocused.

Initially I put in a lot of couch-and-TV time, along with the hours and days of sleep and starvation that accompany depression (part of rebirth). Remember, too, that I was cleaning up a monster mess, which was inhumanly stressful. But ultimately I was concerned with learning and growing and making things right again. I was broke, broken and brokenhearted, and had to find my way out. Looking back on it now, I see that, like most things, the way out was a process.

My reawakening began with four steps.

STEP ONE

First, I got really, really, really angry. While I'm no Mel Gibson, I can get hot, so let's just say there was emotional blood out there on the streets. For a while I was ticked off at everyone. I was just plain pissed at the world. I walked around muttering the same things over and over again like Dustin Hoffman in *Rain Man*. "Screw *him*, screw the *economy*, screw the *lawyers*, screw *you*, this is not *my* fault and don't say it is," and so on, at everyone and no one, as I languished my days away in full-blown victim mode.

The thing is, you can try to BS others but just try to BS yourself. Good luck with that, because your body ain't havin' it. It took two bouts of diverticulitis for me to realize that my poison darts were only poisoning me. Even this early on, I was starting to get inklings that perhaps I had something to do with this whole mess? Moi? Anyway, what was so odd is nobody agreed with me. All my loyal friends were on the of-course-it's-not-your-fault bandwagon, which I see now, was a huge clue that most people are just not self-aware and by habit, thrive in the big dark sea of blame. I guess blame is more fun than accountability. It sure makes for a better story. But blame does not work. Buddha knows best and he has decreed: *Holding onto anger is like drinking poison and expecting the other person to die.*

Well, that seemed pointless, so I guessed it was time to surrender. Once I finally owned up and became accountable, the healing began.

I had to face a basic "duh" moment: If I were going to take responsibility—and credit—for our many victories, so too must I stand up and be responsible—and accountable—for the failures. *I* was the constant in this equation. Me. Nobody else.

I have no idea what my partner's part in all this was because we never talked about it. And I probably never will know, because it doesn't matter. It's not my place to indict anyone else. We all have to look inside ourselves and find our own truth. Mine was that I had to suspend judgment, stop blaming, including the economy and myself, and instead *simply become accountable.* I could feel it—self-awareness was brewing.

WHAT I HAVE LEARNED IS THIS:

BLAME HAS NO POSITIVE OUTCOME. IT'S TOXIC. ACCOUNTABILITY MEANS BEING RESPONSIBLE AND ANSWERABLE. IT'S HEALTHY.

I had to face it: whatever happens to me is my responsibility. Period. I had the power to make this right, just as I had the power to mess it up in the first place. (Clearly I had not used my power wisely.) Why didn't I just simply talk to my partner, without the *Real Housewives of New Jersey* freak out crap, and then really listen to what he had to say? I had not fought to *the death* to keep my partnership, partner, or at least, my friend. I had let everyone down, most of all myself. I had taken bad advice when I knew it was not what I wanted. I had allowed myself to reach this sorry-ass point in life. I had relinquished my power by not being clear about what my power was in the first place.

I, I, I, I.... See the pattern? Wait! There's more.

I had to own my situation, *recognize the truths* in it, and then—and this is hugely important—*forgive myself and everyone involved.* That is accountability. And only then would I have the opportunity to move on and build something stronger, better and more balanced.

Yay! I was starting to grow.

I also had to open myself to the many other lessons I was about to learn and become grateful for what I *did* have. That might sound like a touchy feel-y stretch, but gratitude is the secret ingredient in the healing potion. Try healing without it.

STEP TWO

Next, I got organized. Because I am a brand strategist hooked on process, I created a process to do that. Process is all about being organized; it is a strategy that leads to clarity, which I believe is "it." (I'm sure that's what Curly in *City Slickers* was trying to say when, smiling and peaceful, he raised his index finger toward the sky shortly before he croaked.) Lack of clarity is arguably the #1 cause of stress, arguments and break-ups.

Any process takes time, which requires patience. (You already know

I didn't have much of that.) It also takes discipline, of which I had lots. I was finding a balance.

Everything takes the time it takes. It takes time for a wound to heal; for a potato to grow; for a baby to be born; for the storm to pass; for the brownies

WHAT I HAVE LEARNED IS THIS:

EVERYTHING IS A PROCESS.

to bake. And it takes time to create and maintain a healthy partnership. If you understand that going in, everything becomes easier. If not, you are headed for deep sh*t.

The way back also involved processing grief, because this experience was a death in every way. The death of a dream, a friendship, a business, my confidence, a passion—the death of the old me, losses as final and painful as physical death. Do not minimize this. It is critical to healing.

STEP THREE

Then I got busy. I opened my eyes and ears and, finally, my heart. I was learning that learning happens through listening and being more heart-than head-based. While it's different for everyone, my get-to-know-myself "Rebirth School" curriculum involved much time and many time zones. I spent the next three years in the reflection, education, travel, training, spirituality, reading, teaching, volunteering, crow-eating, apologizing and learning necessary for me to find out how and why I hit this bottom in the first place. Wherever I went, there I was, looking at myself in that big, tell-no-lies mirror. Good hair days notwithstanding, I was not loving what I was seeing.

For different reasons, my travels took me to Mexico, Peru, Ecuador, Scotland, Italy, California, New York, Georgia and North Carolina. I learned from incredible people like Tony Robbins, Seth Godin, Keith

Cunningham, Deepak Chopra, Char Margolis, Michael Smorch, Debbie Ford, April Norris, John Sutton, Phyllis Apple, Brendon Burchard, Harry S. Dent, Dr. Daniel Amen, Arielle Ford, Vicki St. George . . . oh yeah, everybody, meet the amazing Vicki St. George, my partner in writing this book. (See that word *partner*?)

Vicki usually works as a ghostwriter (JustWriteNow.com) but I dogged her to come out from behind the curtain and say yes to co-writing and editing with me. She is a rock-star writing partner, editor and human being. More important than her brilliance with words is her deep understanding of humanity and how people operate. Yes, she helped me create this book, but more importantly, she helped me heal through her insights and encouragement that this book will help others. Thank you, my friend.

Along the way, there were other teachers. They showed up disguised as parents, friends, ex-husbands, children, musicians, lyrics, books, movies, television shows, cats, dogs, butterflies and more. I kept them close, valued them, listened to what they had to tell me and was grateful for their illuminations.

WHAT I HAVE LEARNED IS THIS:

TEACHERS ARE EVERYWHERE. OPEN YOUR HEART AND LISTEN, AND THEY WILL FIND YOU.

Many of you are thinking, "I can't afford to run around the world like that." I couldn't either, but I did it anyway. And you don't have to. Most of the people mentioned above are online and yours for the asking. They are in this world to serve. The rest are in your life already. Plus, you can make anything happen if you are committed. I'm a learning junkie and think of all learning as an investment, not an expense. L'Oreal says you're worth it and you are. If you aren't going to invest in yourself, then who? You'll find the way. And while you're at it, trash the pauper mindset. It's the enemy; it's limiting and destructive to self-esteem. It's also boring—nobody wants to listen to you whine. Just ask my friends and family who listened to me.

Most peoples' lives are about what they cannot afford to do. Mine became about what I cannot afford *not* to do.

STEP FOUR

Finally, I created the Partnersh*t-to-Par+nership process to help others avoid my mistakes. Actually, it pretty much created, or *revealed*, itself in the form of those good questions I referred to earlier. I've already told you that deep pain—and the desire to make things right—are great motivators. The universe will do a data dump into your brain and heart when you are ready ("When the student is ready..."). You'll meet all these questions starting in Section A. In the meantime, here's how it happened.

I had become clear that while we had gone about the business of being in business, we never focused on the business of being *human*, or what it would take to be in a partnership with ourselves *or* each other. So logically, I thought if I could create killer processes that helped my clients define and build their brands with incredible success, why couldn't I figure out how to do that for people who were either potential or current partners? Why couldn't I help people create great partnerships based on self-awareness, acceptance of accountability, shared values, established agreements and clarity around what each partner wanted and needed?

Ha! I had defined a clear, actionable goal, one of the key tools for creating clarity. I was on my way to something good.

I had seen those kinds of partnerships—I knew they existed. I'd read about many of the partners you'll meet in this book: Buffett and Munger, Hilary and Norgay and others. In fact, you could say I became obsessed with partnerships—the moth to the flame, if you will. Thinking about them. Reading about them. Analyzing them. Building one with myself. And just like a divorced woman who looks at her happily and-long-married friends and realizes marital success is possible, I knew that to build that kind of partnership would be worth exerting time, energy and effort. But I also knew one critical thing: that kind of partnership would have to be built on a foundation that was so strong, so unshakeable, so deep, that even the strongest of personal and professional "hurricanes" wouldn't be able to blow it down.

But what was that foundation? Rules? Written agreements? Common business goals? A solid business plan? Even if we had all of that, our partnership would have cratered simply because *we didn't understand our own or each other's basic human wants and needs.* And in my quest to find out what that foundation should be, I discovered nobody was talking about it.

Someone had to. Hmmmmm...

WHAT I HAVE LEARNED IS THIS:

> ## A BUSINESS PARTNERSHIP IS A RELATIONSHIP FIRST, AND BUSINESS SECOND.

A true, lasting partnership, I realized, has to be built on a foundation of self-awareness that takes all of our human foibles, frailties, strengths, and greatness into account, and uses all of it to cement both the partners and the business together. Every great partnership—indeed, every great business, relationship, and friendship—has to be built on a completely human foundation.

Click. Daylight. Cue the choir of angels singing hallelujah!!!!

A Human Foundation.

Holy smokes. That was it. Nobody was talking about that either. Not even the biz school brainiacs.

So that was what had been missing in my partnership: *a shared human foundation for our shared business!*

By God, I thought, *I have something here. This can help people.*

Take my partner and me. Sure, we liked each other and *thought* our skills and goals were compatible. ("Thought " is as deadly a word as assume.) We were like a homesteading couple that finds a likely plot of land and throws up a flimsy house just to get a roof over their heads without taking the time to dig the kind of foundation that would support the house in rough weather. We had been so eager to go into business together that we hadn't taken any time to dig deep into our own humanity—to create the kind of strong relationship with ourselves first, and then each other, that could weather the storms of recession, personal tragedy or increased competition. And without a strong foundation, even the seemingly small "cracks," like incompatible styles and goals (which, as you'll see, are not small at all if they're not addressed), weakened our partnership daily.

I'm not a psychologist or lawyer or financial planner or business school graduate or any of the expected disciplines for this kind of process. I'm just an entrepreneurial person who had a deeply painful, life-changing experience, took the time to go inside and learn why, and wants to help people who want to be in partnerships to take a better path.

WHAT I HAVE LEARNED IS THIS:

A HUMAN FOUNDATION IS THE BASIS UPON WHICH ALL PARTNERSHIPS, BUSINESSES AND OTHER RELATIONSHIPS SHOULD BE BUILT.

IT STARTS WITH YOU BEING IN PARTNERSHIP WITH YOURSELF FIRST.

Evidence? Well, we are all taught to believe that Business = Profit. Certainly that is true, but it is not the only truth and it has to be goal #2. If profit is your only goal, it will bring you down sure as the sun will rise tomorrow. Ever hear of Enron? Lehman Brothers? Merrill Lynch? Maybe you've heard of the United States of America, where collective greed including government, the Federal Reserve, bankers, mortgage companies, investors, small businesses and yes, everyday citizens, crashed our economy?

WHAT I HAVE LEARNED IS THIS:

BUSINESS 3 PEOPLE.

Becoming self-aware, knowing your vision and then partnering with good people who align with that vision has to be goal #1. A partner business—actually, any business—has to be about people first and foremost. Profit follows.

Before we get into building the Human Foundation, however, there are some things we need to clear up about partnerships in general. There are a lot of misconceptions, misunderstandings, and downright lies about the good and the bad of sharing your business life with a partner. And since your Human Foundation had better be built on good, solid, common ground if it's going to have any chance of lasting, let's do a little digging to clear away any mental "dirt."

PART TWO

IT'S ABOUT TIME SOMEBODY TOLD THE TRUTH ABOUT PAR1NERSHIPS

4

WHY A PARTNERSHIP?

Two are better than one, because they have a good return for their labor:
If either of them falls down, one can lift up the other.
But pity anyone who falls and has no one to help them up.
—Ecclesiastes 4:9-10

Before you consider getting into one, you might want to know: What exactly is a partnership? Let's poke around and see what people are saying.

A **partnership** *is the relationship existing between two or more persons who join to carry on a trade or business.* —**The Internal Revenue Service**

A **partnership** *is an arrangement where parties agree to cooperate to advance their mutual interests.* —**Wikipedia**

partnership *[pahrt-ner-ship].noun 1. the state or condition of being a partner; participation; association; joint interest.* —**Dictionary.com**

Partnership. *An association of two or more persons engaged in a business enterprise in which the profits and losses are shared proportionally. The legal definition of a partnership is generally stated as "an association of two or more persons to carry on as co-owners a business for profit."* —**Revised Uniform Partnership Act § 101 [1994].**

*A **partnership** is a single business where two or more people share own-ership.* —**Small Business Administration**

Partnership. *A type of unincorporated business organization in which multiple individuals called general partners manage the business and are equally liable for its debts.* —**Investorwords.com**

Partnership. *A type of business organization in which two or more in-dividuals pool money, skills, and other resources, and share profit and loss in accordance with terms of the Partnership Plan. In absence of such agreement, a partnership is assumed to exist where the participants in an enterprise agree to share the associated risks and rewards proportionately.* —**Business Dictionary**

Partnership. The mutual business. *Ok, Joe. Look here. We three rob that damned bank. Share for three? No that's bad. Kill the third. Then, we kill another. And no need to share! I will call it . . . Partnership.* —**Urban Dictionary**

No wonder we have a partnership problem in this country. Sure, partnerships are serious legal and financial entities, but do any of these definitions mention any relationship you might have with *yourself?* Do they say anything at all about how people feel, what they need, want or will give to *each other?* Is there any human consciousness at work here? Any self-awareness? Not so much.

(That Urban Dictionary definition is classic, by the way. At least that guy knows what he wants and isn't afraid to say it.)

What does partnership mean to *you?* Likely it's an amalgam of the above. I believe it has to mean more. I can promise you this: Your defi-nition will change once you do the Partnersh*t-to-Par+nership Process. You will never look at yourself or your partner the same way again. That's a good thing.

Now that I know better, here's my definition. Like the partnership itself, it's a work in progress:

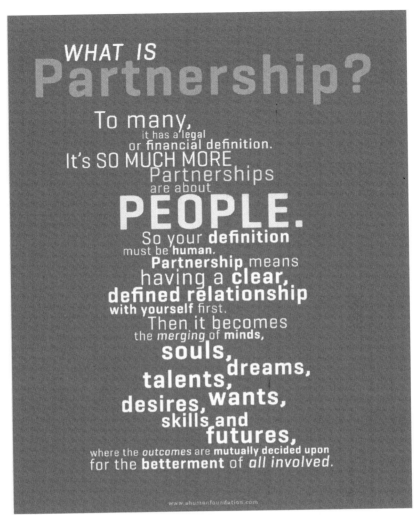

Figure 4.1 *Partnership Definition*

Partnerships are no small part of our culture. Says Inc. Magazine, "The number of business partnerships in the U.S. has been growing steadily by an annual rate of about 5.6 percent a year to more than 3 million in 2007, according to the most recent records reported by the U.S. Internal Revenue Service. The total net income for these partnerships has also been on the rise, increasing by 2.5 percent from 2006 to a total of $683 billion for 2007, IRS figures show." Yet, the Small Business Administration reported in 2009 that nearly 51 percent of new businesses fail by the time they reached the 5-year mark.

While not all these failed businesses are partnerships, it is likely those numbers have only increased, given the state of our economy. Some of this is preventable. The resulting financial, legal and health burden on this country is tremendous and one we can no longer bear. We have to change the mindset of people going into partnerships. Wake up people! We have all been focused on the wrong thing. It's you first, people foremost, and *then* business.

You may have noticed that things are not going so well right now. This is an opportunity! According to the Kaufmann Foundation President and CEO Carl Schramm, entrepreneurs have led the US out of every recession for the past 100 years. The country is reinventing itself and needs good, strong, idea-based, innovative businesses to remain competitive. Small businesses are also the cornerstone of America and create 75 percent of new jobs (or did, until we imploded—the jury is still out on new stats). I expect that number to grow larger in this new economy. And since partnerships are the cornerstone of entrepreneurial small businesses, it's time to reinvent the partnership as well.

GREAT PARTNERSHIPS 3 GREATNESS

You already know how my partnership story ends. So you might still think that after such a disaster, I should run screaming for the hills (hard to do in Florida) and foreswear all human contact. Nothing could be further from the truth.

I still believe that nothing really great ever happens alone (nope, not even THAT). Former Disney CEO Michael Eisner wrote a very cool "why" book about partnerships called *Working Together: Why Great Partnerships Succeed.* While the prevailing attitude on partnerships is that they're more trouble than they're worth, he feels the opposite. He believes in partnership.

"I think that people who do it only alone ... tend to get in trouble,"

Eisner said. "Being in the foxhole with somebody ... when things go bad, you've got somebody to talk to. When things go well, you've got somebody to high five."

Human beings are biologically driven to collaborate, and not just to propagate the species: the only way our caveman ancestors managed to make it through the Ice Age was by banding together to hunt and gather and huddle around that very first campfire. And Daniel Boone, Davy Crockett, Jim Bowie, and all those intrepid solo pioneers of the Wild West to the contrary, one man against the wilderness usually meant a quick death. Hell, even the "Lone" Ranger was smart enough to keep Tonto by his side.

In business, however, we've fallen victim to the "Lone Ranger" mythology. We kowtow to the Superstar CEO/Business Founder, who creates a billion-dollar company through the application of his or her genius. Or so we think. If you look deeper into the legends of those business giants, you'll find almost all of them had help. It was the Walton *brothers*—Sam and Bud—who founded Wal-Mart together in 1962. Both Bill Gates and Steve Jobs had Paul Allen and Steve Wozniak. (Bill Gates once said, "I've never done anything solo, except take tests.") And Larry Page and Sergey Brin produced one of the most dominant companies in the world: Google.

The great "solo" success in business is usually a myth. I'm hard-pressed to find even one example for this book. Truthfully, partnership, collaboration and strategic alliance are where successful businesses are moving today. Visionary businesses focus on developing relationships and

WHAT I HAVE LEARNED IS THIS:

COMPANIES FINALLY UNDERSTAND THAT BUSINESS IS SIMPLY THE INTERRELATIONSHIP OF HUMAN BEINGS.

even partnerships with customers, employees, suppliers, even regulators and government where possible. Instead of hierarchy, there's equality. Instead of top-down leadership, there's partnership.

I for one am glad to see the change. Even though my last business partnership crashed and burned, I still believe that partnerships are the best thing for business since double-entry bookkeeping. I'm writing this book with Vicki. Could I have done it alone? Sure. Would it be as good? No way.

WHAT I HAVE LEARNED IS THIS:

YOUR PARTNERSHIP IS AN EXTENSION OF YOU. IT'S A REFLECTION OF YOU.

Would you invite your friends over to a messy, dirty, chaos-stricken house? Would you date someone who embarrassed you? Would you send your children out into the world acting like selfish, naughty brats? Not if you valued yourself. So, then, why would you ever allow your partnership to become that? Or allow yourself to enter into a partnership that is wrong for you?

The best way to avoid all this and protect your partnerships is to be very clear before you start why you should take on a partner or partners in your business—and ultimately, whether partnership is right for you at all.

+ + + + + + +

12 GREAT REASONS FOR PARTNERSHIP

Here are 12 good reasons for entering into a partnership. Many of these were true for me; see if any of them speak to you.

1. **Two heads are better than one (mostly).**

   The Coen Brothers. Frank and Orville Wright. Dave Packard and Bill Hewlett. Larry and Sergey. Rocky and Bullwinkle—well maybe not them. But in most cases, having a great partner can multiply the amount of ideas, intelligence, background, and experience your business can draw upon. We all need a good wingman or -woman.

2. **You can double your resources and your ability to reach customers.**

   This was us. When I was running my business plan/RFP business, I was continually contracting with local design companies to help create with the visual elements of branding. My partner had worked as a graphic designer at one such firm, and when that company lost its creative director he started up his own solo design service. I kept giving him design work, and eventually the penny dropped: why didn't we just combine forces and start our own branding business? He could supervise all the design work, and I would be the marketing and client outreach person. He had graphics skills; I had business, sales, writing and branding acumen, plus a killer Rolodex. (Yes, it was still the Rolodex days, although electronic databases soon took over.) Together we could offer a much wider range of services to a much larger number of clients.

   Bringing in a partner can give you access to a much richer pool of financial resources and business networks. And because there are two of you, there's someone else to hit the pavements and look for business, cultivate clients, network and ultimately serve your customers.

3. **Your partner has strengths that you lack, and vice versa.**

Batman and Robin, the Fantastic Four, the Avengers—even superheroes band together to compensate for each other's weaknesses so that individually they can focus on using their strengths. That's what great partners do. As collaborators Rodd Wagner and Gale Muller write in *Power of 2*, "Your strengths are stronger and your weaknesses weaker than you realize. You need help. You are also precisely the help someone else needs."

4. **There's someone else to rely on when it comes to bringing home the bacon.**

After my partner and I went into business together, we could take on a lot more projects than before. In next to no time, our business exploded. Most partners will tell you that having someone else to help shoulder the workload or just take responsibility for different parts of the business can increase your company's income potential dramatically.

5. **It promotes greater creativity and can spur innovation.**

It's hard to brainstorm alone. Most people's creative juices flow more freely if they can bounce ideas off others. And things get *really* interesting when you have partners who bring their own ideas and perspectives to the party—that's often when the biggest leaps of innovation occur. I know I'm far more creative in the kind of "give and take" atmosphere that my business had at its best.

6. **It serves as a model for employees and fosters collaboration.**

The old top-down business model is dead. I've been to the funeral. Nowadays smart businesses are looking to "partner" with employees and other people at all levels to hear their ideas, get their input and even empower them to make decisions that in the past might have been run up the corporate ladder. And partnerships at the top of the business can serve as collaborative models for the rest of the company. (This is a benefit that can swing both ways, however. If the partners are great collaborators, employees will model them; if there's trouble in paradise, employees will model that, too.)

7. **A partner's perspective can help you break free of your old way of doing things.**

Brothers Sam, Harry, Albert, and Jack Warner founded the Warner Bros. movie studios in 1918. When Sam Warner proposed the radical idea of synchronizing sound with their movies, brother Harry opposed the idea, saying, "Who the hell wants to hear actors talk?" But Sam persevered and in 1927, Warner Bros. made film history with *The Jazz Singer*, the first "talking picture." Sam's perspective on the possibilities of sound in film liberated an entire industry from its old ways and put Warner Bros. back in the black and back on the map. Sometimes it takes another person's perspective to shake a successful business out of complacency and see an old business in a new way.

8. **Partners can help you take greater risks.**

A good partner can challenge you to take the kinds of risk that will help your business grow. When things were going right in my partnership, we were able to take on projects that were way outside our respective comfort zones. We felt safe enough to say, "Sure, we can do that," when we didn't have a clue how to actually do it. That was one of my favorite parts of our partnership. I knew we could master just about anything together. It was so much fun!

Partners also can encourage each other to be more daring simply because each partner figures the other will be there to pick up the pieces if the risk doesn't pan out. When Sir Edmund Hilary and Tenzing Norgay set out to climb Mt. Everest in 1953, relied on the other for keeping both of them safe despite the massive risks of climbing the world's tallest mountain. At one point, Hilary broke through soft snow and slid into a crevasse. But because he and Tenzing were roped together, Tenzing was able to stop Hilary's fall and pull him to safety. Great partners help you attempt big things and pull you out when things go wrong.

9. **Partners also can serve as a restraint in keeping you from risking too much.**

One of the reasons Warren Buffett has partnered with Charlie Munger for almost 50 years is the fact that Charlie says no to most investment opportunities that come their way. "When I call Charlie with an idea," says Buffet, "he has three reactions. One is, 'Warren, that's a dumb idea.' Then, we put one hundred percent of our net worth into the idea. If it's 'Warren, that's one of the dumbest ideas I've ever heard,' we put half of our net worth into the idea. And if it's 'You've gone out of your mind, and I'm going to have you committed,' then we pass." Warren is an incredible enthusiast; Charlie is the bath of cold water that stops Warren from doing something stupid with Berkshire Hathaway's money. A good partner will tell you when an idea is full of crap and keep you from taking on too much risk.

10. **Working together for a common goal is a lot more fun than working alone.**

In the same way that great sex is a lot more fun with a partner, business is a lot more fun when you can share it with someone else. When my partnership was good, every day at work was so much fun I actually hated having to go home. (So we didn't! Instead, we took the whole team to dinner.) There's something exciting and exhilarating in facing challenges together, and if you're blessed with a partner with a sense of humor that meshes with yours (and I was), work becomes like play.

11. **Try playing good cop/bad cop when it's just you.**

Managing clients and employees is exhausting. On the days when you just need a break, your partner is there to pick up the slack. Or if you have a difficult client on the phone and you're not in the frame of mind to reason rather than react, your partner can take over. Our synergy was good in this area. When I was overwhelmed, I could always count on my partner to listen with an unfathomable amount of patience. Sometimes you need to punt to win.

12. **It sucks to cry or celebrate alone.**

Think about getting the big contract or hearing that your loan has been called, with no one else there. Somehow jumping around screaming with happiness by yourself isn't nearly as great as jumping with a partner. Conversely, when the sh*t hits the fan, there's nothing like having a shoulder available when you need it, and providing one when they do. Having someone to share the highs and lows of business makes both better.

So much for great reasons. But just like going into marriage for the wrong reasons will lead to massive pain and expense, going into a business partnership for the wrong reasons can wreck you both emotionally and financially. The following six lousy reasons to go into partnership will gain you not a partner, but a ball and chain. If you find yourself under the influence of any of these reasons, don't walk—run, run, run, run, run, away from the partnership.

6 LOUSY REASONS TO GO INTO PARTNERSHIP

1. **Fear**

This reminds me of the people who get married because they're afraid they'll end up old and alone. Some people are simply too scared to go into business by themselves so they glom onto a partner. Fear comes from not knowing yourself and not having defined outcomes. So if you don't, then don't. Business is tough, with or without a partner, and you'd better be ready for it. If you're scared without a partner, you'll still be scared with one. Get over it, or don't get into business.

2. Money (or lack of it)

Maybe you don't have enough money to get your business launched, and someone suggests to you that you bring in what are called "equity" partners—meaning, people who have money and are willing to put it into your business in return for an ownership stake. Now, I'm never going to tell anyone they shouldn't put money into a business. In fact, I believe that any business owner should have a significant amount of skin in the game, whether that "skin" is financial, intellectual or any other resource you can name. But if the fact that a prospective partner has money they're willing to invest in the business is the primary reason for the relationship, you're setting yourself up for more problems than the money may be worth.

Remember me telling you about the importance of knowing your partner's financial philosophy? Do not forget this advice. In most people's minds, more money equals more power. Therefore, unless you are willing to be a junior partner, or you have assets that are equal to the capital this person will invest—and the investor also sees those assets as equal—you're selling control of your business to someone else.

3. Need

There's a big difference between *wanting* a partner and *needing* a partner. Whenever we do things out of need, our thinking, evaluating minds can go out the window and we grab the first person whom we think has those particular skills or assets. Problem is, we're likely to choose partners that might work well in the short term but not in the long. If you "need" a partner, see if you can get what you "need" by hiring it, contracting for it, or bringing in a consultant. Need is a lousy basis for any relationship, much less a business partnership. Yes, you'll be closer to your business partners than you are with 99 percent of the other people in your life. But in any relationship, if you go into it because you *need* a partner for something, then you're likely to find yourself knee-deep in partnersh*t all too soon.

4. **Peer Pressure**

    Maybe you're getting ready to start a business or grow the one you currently have, and well-intentioned friends say, "Whoa, that's a lot for you to take on by yourself! Are you sure you have the skills or resources to handle this? If you try it solo, you might lose it all. Don't risk everything by yourself. Get a partner! Get investors! It's the prudent thing to do . . . " Your friends may be giving you great advice—but not if their advice is the *only* reason you consider taking on a partner. In the same way you don't want your kids to succumb to peer pressure when it comes to smoking, drinking, or drugs, don't let yourself be pressured into partnership if it doesn't suit your personality or your business goals.

5. **"Golden Opportunity"**

    You're working along somewhere (in your own business or for someone else) either happily or not, and you receive an offer to become someone's business partner. This "golden opportunity" may be extraordinarily flattering and extremely tempting, even if you prefer to work on your own or like the security of a big company, and you may decide to jump at the chance without much thought. But today's "golden opportunity" can be tomorrow's lead-lined coffin unless the partnership fits your goals, personality, work style and so on. Make sure the opportunity is truly "golden" for your life.

6. Common Interest

You both love love love kites! You dream kites, build kites, fly kites, whatever . . . and that passion just has to translate into a great partnership, right? I mean, who else but the two of you could make this business soar?

Well, whether it's kites, cars, a cleaning service or handbags, mutual passion is only one piece of the puzzle. You must have a mutual vision and passion for so much more than just the product or it won't work.

WHAT I HAVE LEARNED IS THIS:

A BUSINESS PARTNERSHIP IS A HUMAN RELATIONSHIP. IT WILL BECOME A VERY INTENSE, EMOTIONAL, CREATIVE AND FINANCIALLY INTIMATE ENTITY VERY QUICKLY.

You'd darn well better understand why you're going into partnership, what you want from it, and what you're willing to give to it, right from the start.

Most of all, you'd better not let yourself be deceived by the various lies people will tell you about the benefits of partnership. More on that next.

5

BEFORE YOU GET A PARTNER, GET REAL: THE LIES AND TRUTHS OF PARTNERSHIP

People do not believe lies because they have to, but because they want to.
—Malcolm Muggeridge

I know women who went into marriage all dewy-eyed and vowing that they'd never part. I'll admit I went into my business partnership the same way—completely blinded by the excitement and promise of success. Even when my partner and I were obviously done, I was still hanging on by my fingernails, thinking we'd have our Dr. Phil moment of reconciliation. Instead, when we finally closed our doors, it felt like we'd spent eons beating each other up on the Jerry Springer show.

Partnersh*it is built on lies. I'm not talking about just the lies that some partners actually tell each other (that alone will destroy a partnership), but more insidiously, the ass-umptions, thoughts, fairy tales and outright fallacies that people believe. While intentions might be good, these are lies, plain and simple.

Take it from me: it's far better to be absolutely clear about what partnership really is and is not, long before you open your heart and doors to another person or sign on the dotted line. Think of this as your Partnersh*t Intervention: it starts by telling the truth and busting the lies once and for all.

Take a look at this list and see if you've thought about or believed any of these. Then read the cold, hard truth that's based on the experience of people like me who have been buried by partnersh*t.

LIE #1

Business partnerships are about business.

> TRUTH: Get real: partnerships are always relationships first and businesses second. If the relationship isn't working, the business will go down the drain. If the business is going down the drain, a good relationship between partners may be the only thing that can save it. That's why smart partners work as hard and consistently in developing their communication skills and interpersonal abilities as they do their business skills.

LIE #2

The best partners are people you already know intimately—that is, family, friends, or colleagues.

> TRUTH: Have you ever had a colleague get promoted at work and all of a sudden she becomes Ms. "Captain Bligh"? Or perhaps you went on a road trip with your easygoing cousin only to discover that his idea of a vacation is driving 12 hours straight through and peeing into a bottle to avoid having to stop? You may think you know someone intimately, but you may be shocked to discover that they become totally different in another context. Even though you "know" someone, you can't ass-ume that you know what kind of business partner he or she will be. As John

D. Rockefeller put it, "A friendship founded on business is a good deal better than a business founded on friendship."

LIE #3
Your partner is you in another body.

> TRUTH: Oh please—you should have gotten over this one after your first crush in junior high school. People are different, and the fact that you're in a partnership with someone will only bring their different needs, drives and behaviors to the forefront. If you expect your partner to be just like you, to want what you want, or act as you'd act, you're not ready for a partnership (or a relationship of any kind, for that matter).

LIE #4
Because a partnership is a business, you don't necessarily have to understand (or even like) your business partner.

> TRUTH: It's guaranteed that there will be times you won't understand or like your partner, but you'd better make it a priority to figure out how you can do both—most of the time, anyway. One of the reasons I created the Partnersh*t to Par+nership Process is to help people who were thinking about going into business together understand each other at a very deep level, so that in those moments when you ask, "What was he/she thinking?!?!" you can actually figure it out. You need to do your best to understand what drives your partner and even more so, yourself, while at the same time recognizing that, given the pressures of business and life, human beings will surprise you every time. And you'd darn well better like the other person; otherwise you're going to be fundamentally miserable every moment you're together.

LIE #5

We won't let any personal issues affect our partnership (or partnership issues affect our personal lives).

> TRUTH: How many different ways can I say it: BUSINESS IS PERSONAL. Period. No one can separate the two. So be prepared for both you and your partner to bring your personal troubles to your business whether you want to or not. Conversely, a toxic partnership will make its way home to your marriage or other relationship.

LIE #6

Partners should approach business in the same way. Disagreements kill a partnership.

> TRUTH: You should be in agreement on basic principles, certainly, but just because someone does things their own way doesn't make him or her wrong. In fact, it makes the soup richer. Just get some agreement in advance on how you're going to deal with any future differences.

LIE #7

You can trust your partner wholeheartedly.

> TRUTH: I wish, but truth be told, you can usually trust your partner to surprise you with what they do or say. The old nuclear treaty that was based on "trust but verify" kept the U.S. and the U.S.S.R from blowing each other up for decades. The same principle can help keep your partnership from a nuclear meltdown.

LIE #8

There's no hierarchy or "boss" in a partnership, and roles and titles

don't matter.

TRUTH: Bull. Roles and titles are some of the most important things to clarify—they delineate what each partner will be responsible for and what they have authority to do. Great partners are complementary: they don't duplicate each other's efforts. Instead, they are strong where their partner is weak and vice versa. Without a hierarchy or defined roles, you end up with a mess—a lot of ass-umptions about who's responsible for what, pissed-off people ("I thought you were handling that!"), and wasted effort. You'd *better* get clear about roles and titles long before you become partners. And remember: there is only *one* boss.

LIE #9
Your partner will work as hard as you will.

TRUTH: Maybe, but maybe not—and their definition of "hard work" might not be the same as yours. One person's "working hard" may be dreaming up a list of potential clients or spending hours creating an org chart, while yours might be customer service, client meetings, balancing the books or doing something that brings cash in the door. In actual fact, all of these activities are good for the business, but unless you feel your partner is contributing and you respect that contribution, it's going to be a problem.

LIE #10
Your partner shares your goals.

TRUTH: How would you know unless you ask? And, by the way, do you even *know* what your goals are? Sure, you both may want a successful business, but what does "successful" mean? You may be looking to build something you can sell in ten years, but your partner sees the business as a cash machine that will provide abundant income now—two very different goals. You must get *really* clear about both your goals, compare them to reach some kind of consensus and then revisit them frequently as the business shifts to make sure you're still aligned.

LIE #11

You always have each other's backs.

TRUTH: In the very times when you want your partner to have your back, he or she may desert you out of self-preservation. (People do weird things when they're stressed or when they feel livelihood or identity threatened.) Even in more general circumstances, like presenting a united front to employees or clients, you can't always count on your partner to back you up. The Partnersh*t to Par+nership Process will focus you and your partner on setting rules in advance for how you will support each other and handle disagreements.

LIE #12

You can't do this without each other.

TRUTH: Remember the line from the movie, *Jerry Maguire*? "You… complete me…." Well, that had better not be true in your partnership. You may be better and stronger together; you may have complementary strengths and backgrounds and both love dogs and pizza and I don't know what else. But nobody completes you except you. I've already talked to you about this "need" nonsense. Save your "needing" for a hot bath or a margarita. If you feel you can't be in business without a partner, or this partner in particular, you probably aren't strong enough to be in business at all.

LIE #13

Partners don't need a written agreement—a handshake is good enough. You can fill in the details as you go along.

TRUTH: And how many thousands of partners find themselves in court suing each other? There are a million good reasons for spelling things out in a written Partnership Plan, and at least a dollar attached to each reason. You cannot hug or handshake your way to partnership success. I recommend that people have both a legal agreement and another, separate Human Foundation-based partnership document that spells out all the human aspects of the partnership covered in the Partnersh*t-to-Par+nership Process. Putting things in writing will take time up front. Do the work. It will save you time, money and heartache throughout the life of the partnership. You do not want to mess around here, and no, signing your corporate papers is not enough. You wouldn't hire an employee without an agreement, so why on earth would you take on a partner without one? If you don't have this document, the judge gets to decide. One of you will not like the decision.

LIE #14

Money in the partnership doesn't matter all that much. What matters is that the business is successful.

TRUTH: People use money as a measure of a lot of things that have nothing to do with dollars and cents. People equate the amount they're paid to their value, contribution, prestige and selfworth. Every partner in the world will measure his or her compensation against what the other partners are earning and make judgments about each person's relative value to the business. I remember a situation at my partner's old agency, where the 20-year partners fought that status with dueling Mercedes'—they had to outdo each other in every way. They ended up hating each other and breaking up. Money does matter—not just financially but mentally and emotionally. So you might as well recognize the fact and deal with it as part of your partnership preparation.

LIE #15
You will split everything equally, including workload and finances.

TRUTH: Hello? A "50/50 partnership" or any version of an equal split creates deadlock or stalemate. It's also a completely fictional division. No relationship of any kind—friendship, marriage, or business—is equal. Each partner will bring different skills and assets to the business, and will have different needs and commitments. This will affect both finances and workload. Trying to keep things equal is probably the least fair division any partnership can have. Instead, divide ownership, finances and workload based on (1) skills, (2) assets, and ultimately (3) an agreed-upon outline that takes each partner's unique talents and contributions into account.

LIE #16
Once you've got your partnership structure set, there's no more work to be done.

TRUTH: Yeah… and once you walk down the aisle you don't have to work on your marriage. Here's what's real: you'll be fine-tuning your relationship with yourself and your partner constantly. Forget the take-for-granted thing. It won't work at home, and it won't work at the office. *A partnership is a continuing negotiation between expectations and reality.* Your partnership structure is but a starting point and guideline for your legal and actual relationship. Expect it to be challenged and amended consistently.

LIE #17
Your partner will always put you first.

> TRUTH: Really? And you'll always do the same for your partner? Come on… when the sh*t hits the fan it's usually every man or woman for themselves. Even when things are going well it's rare to find a partner who will put another's interests ahead of his or her own. You don't want that. Such people are not likely to contribute much to the partnership anyway. A little self-interest is healthy. Look for partners who will take your interests into account along with theirs, and make sure you do the same. That way, when they win, you win, and vice versa. And give up having expectations. All they get you is upset. Instead, have defined goals and outcomes.

LIE #18
There's no competition in a partnership.

> TRUTH: Hah! If you and/or your partner are competitive people, why would you think you wouldn't compete in a partnership? Partners compete all the time over issues big and small: Who's got the best office. Who's bringing in the best clients. Who makes the most. Who has the best ideas. Who saves the company the most money. Who scores the most runs at the company softball game. Instead of denying your competitive nature, it's better to bring the competition out into the open and use it to your advantage. Competition is healthy. Use it to grow your company.

LIE #19
If one becomes more successful, the other will cheer.

> TRUTH: There's a reason jealousy and envy are two of the seven deadly sins: they're a natural if unattractive tendency in our nature. If partners are competitive (see above), it's normal for one to

be at least a little jealous of the other's success and/or envious of their greater billings or reputation or salary. To paraphrase an old commercial, don't fight Mother Nature. Accept that occasionally there will be feelings of jealousy and envy in your partnership. Better to accept them than deny their existence and let them fester.

LIE #20
Yes, Sonny and Cher broke up, but we never will.

TRUTH: A business partnership isn't a "death 'til us part" marriage (and look how many of those don't make it either). Every story has a beginning, middle and end. So even if you're still making beautiful melodies together 20 or 30 years from now, you will break up at some point. Eventually one of you will sell out, or you'll mutually decide to dissolve the partnership, or one will retire or pass the business along to a family member. Or you will die. And why should your family have to clean up your mess? Nothing lasts forever, even the good stuff. Even the Stones will have to stop touring—sometime!

LIE #21
When it's over, you will shake hands, split everything and move on.

TRUTH: Before or after you cry? Sure, in your Partnership Plan you will spell out exactly how you will dissolve your partnership equitably. But even if you follow your agreement to the letter, you can't spell out how you both will feel about leaving the partnership. Whether closing down is the best idea since sliced bread or an unexpected catastrophe, you and your partner will be dealing with the emotional consequences of your parting ways. The death of your partnership is a loss, and like any other death, you will need to heal from it before you blithely move on to something new.

Interventions are a hard but necessary first step to healing. I know I'm not the only one who has believed one or more (many, many more) of these lies when it comes to creating a healthy, lasting partnership. But building anything on a lie is the first brick in the foundation, not of partnership, but partnersh*t. Understanding the truth—even uncomfortable truth—about partnership is the only solid foundation. You should welcome it. The truth is your friend.

PART THREE

BUILDING A HUMAN FOUNDATION

6

THE PARTNERSH*T-TO-PAR1NERSHIP PROCESS UNFOLDS

Partnership is a process, not a transaction.
—Terry McElroy, SVP, McLane Company

Once I cleared away all the sh*t and understood the truth about both my partnership and myself, I was able to see the unmistakable value of building a Human Foundation. It was at that point the Partnersh*t-to-Par+nership Process started to emerge.

I'd love to say this process just magically revealed itself with no pain or delusion busting, but that would be a lie. And you know how I feel about lies by now. I already told you about how I had to come to terms with my accountability before I could move on or create anything new. Then I had to look at the relationship between partnership and business for what it is and what it isn't.

Companies, good and bad, can, do and will go out of business all the time, for lots of reasons besides partnership breakups. There are economic conditions, shifts in technology, obsolescence of industries, bad management, bad products and even bad weather. Most of these things are *beyond our control,* no matter how good the partnership might be. But now, after personal experience and many priceless lessons, **I believe that not having a rock-solid Human Foundation is the number one *controllable* reason for a partnership business failure.**

For a good business partnership to survive and thrive, I realized that partners must master these 7 areas:

1. Characterization

You Must Define who you both are, first and foremost. Become conscious about how you're wired, what motivates you, what stops you, your energy imprint, your personal goals and desires, thoughts, values, ideals and the viewfinder through which you see the world.

2. Collaboration

You Must Uncover your partnership potential, skills, talents, weaknesses, expectations, determination and ambitions.

3. Communication

You Must State your case. There is nothing more important than good communication. It takes practice. Are you the loudest person in the room or quiet as a mouse? Are you verbal or non? What is your character, temperament, threshold, coping ability? Do you listen? How do you see yourself? Do others agree?

4. Compensation

You Must Ask for what you want. You must be clear about exactly what you are looking for in both the partnership and the business.

What will you bring to it and what will you take? Compensation is much more than just money. Declare what you need for your lifestyle, work style, rewards and eventual exit.

5. Contribution

You Must Give. Are you community-minded and supportive? This is an area that can cause great harm to a partnership if there is no alignment. Uncover the reasons why you are or are not willing to contribute. Knowing this about yourself will serve you in all areas. Giving gets.

6. Construction

You Must Build your business in the same orderly fashion that you build your partnership. This section requires tangible, strategic thoughts, ideas and definition of tactics so you can set goals, outcomes and measurement criteria. Once you have constructed your goals and outcome framework, you'll have what you need to begin the next step, which is creating the business.

7. Creation

You Must Create! Ah, this is the fun part! If you have come this far and are still here, you are finally ready to create your business. Creation is different from building. Think of the analogy of building a house: You *build* the framework on a rock-solid foundation. Then you get to *create* the design, colors, textures, sounds and so on—in other words, the details. Both are critical, and each needs the other to be complete. It's the same with a business. So in this section we will get down to details including your business, branding and marketing plans.

Once I got clear on all of this, voila! The P²P Process was born. I cheered, screamed, and jumped on the couch á la Tom Cruise. I had discovered the **Real Beginning**, the point from which all partnership businesses need to start. I was eager to share these riches with the world.

This process starts with a very simple question: What if?

What If . . .?

You *start* from the REAL BEGINNING:

- Before you commit to a partner
- Before you order the logo-and-a-website special
- Before you buy or lease equipment and office space
- Before you write the business plan
- Before you write the branding and marketing plans
- Before you look for financing
- Before you hire anyone
- Before you start the hunt for clients
- Before you advertise
- Before you launch

And What If . . . ?

You *stop* problems before they begin by:

- Getting to know yourself
- Declaring who you are and what you want
- Exploring the ins and outs of partnerships
- Deciding if partnership is right for you

- Deciding what kind of partnership is right for you

- Knowing how to choose a partner who suits you

- Doing the work necessary for becoming a good partner

- Setting the partner-biz mission, vision and goals

- Creating an atmosphere of open communication

- Understanding that partnerships need attention every day

- Knowing how to manage your partnership

- Learning from and about your partnership

- Planning an exit strategy

- Realizing when it's time to move on

And What If . . .?

You *restart* a partnership or business that's in a growth or troubled phase, from the REAL BEGINNING:

- Before your anger gets the best of you

- Before you put your health and finances at risk

- Before you call the lawyers

- Before you hurt yourself and others

- Before you spend more money

- Before you destroy absolutely everything you worked so hard to achieve

Finally, What If . . .?

The REAL BEGINNING is simply about being human? And doing what human beings must do to achieve clarity? Like:

- Becoming conscious

- Becoming self-aware
- Becoming accountable
- Talking amongst your imperfect selves
- Asking questions
- Answering honestly
- Listening
- Suspending judgment
- Declaring your idea, yourself, your values, your strengths, your weaknesses and your intentions with candor
- Saying exactly what you do and do not want
- Speaking to one another other in simple language that everyone can understand

This is how you create your very *human* foundation, and it sustains absolutely everything you do. A Human Foundation is you first, other people next and then everything else.

WHAT I HAVE LEARNED IS THIS:

> YOU ARE THE FOUNDATION FOR YOUR HUMAN FOUNDATION.
> PEOPLE ARE THE FOUNDATION FOR EVERYTHING.

I swear this is as simple an idea as the Post-It Note. Think of the business as the paper and your foundation as the glue.

Here's how most entrepreneurs and small business owners
build their businesses.

Are you seeing any people in this mix?

Figure 6.1   *Outdated method of building a business*

Here's what makes sense to me.

Figure 6.2   *Building a Human Foundation from the ground up.*

Starting at the ***real beginning*** rearranges the old model and builds from
the only foundation that can create endurance and longevity:

A Human Foundation

Building a Human Foundation helps you and your partner(s) uncover:

- Who you are
- What you stand for
- Why you are here
- What you want
- How you will get it

You are ultimately looking for strategic and emotional alignment, i.e., *trust, collaboration and agreement*, in these areas:

Figure 6.3   *Alignment Model*

What Is the Value of the Human Factor in Your Partnership/Business?

Just stop and think about it for a minute. Say you have a killer business plan, a sexy brand, cool offices and you are marketing your fool head off to your dream clients—but you hate going to work every day because you cannot stand your partner?

Or, you have a really fab product launch coming up; you are insanely focused and busy doing your part of the launch and ass-ume your partner is doing hers. But because you have never talked about it, you don't know that she has absolutely no clue how to upload the correct files, so you not only miss your launch dates but your affiliates get screwed too.

Get the picture?

And how many dollars are frittered away each year by people who open a partner-biz with their heads tucked up their you-know-where's? I don't know the answer to that, but I can tell you that the dollars I lost could have fed a small village somewhere on this planet.

How Do You Measure Your Human Foundation?

Measurement is critical. So the better question might be "How *don't* you?" You can start with dollars if you'd like, but to get to the big bucks a better place to start is with things like clarity; alignment; emotional, spiritual and physical health; joy; purpose; connection; compassion; service; and longevity.

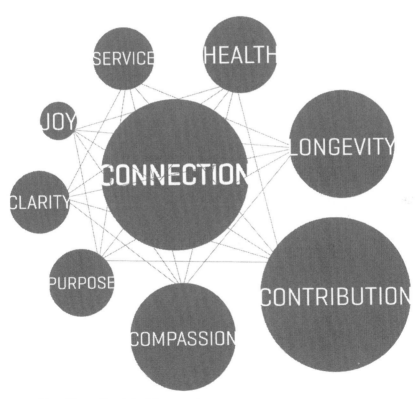

Figure 6.4   *Human Foundation Measurement*

You determine the degree of each, based on your business, branding, marketing and life strategies.

Isn't it nice to be aware and in charge of your own life for a change?

How Do You Use It?

You will use your Human Foundation to:

- Make informed decisions
- Declare and manage expectations
- Manage activities
- Manage resources
- Identify collaborators
- Define success
- Hire
- Expand

- Create goals
- Team build
- Innovate
- Manage employees
- Define measurement
- Create accountability
- Plan exit strategies

Your Human Foundation will be built on the seven areas of mastery, which are the basis for the Partnersh*t-to-Par+nership Process.

Think of the Partnersh*t-to-Par+nership Process as premarital counseling for your business. When it comes to choosing the person or persons you want to spend a large part of your business life with, you'd better get to know them intimately, deeply and comprehensively, to make sure you are truly compatible in the areas that really matter. (I sound like an eHarmony commercial, but it's true.) Only once you establish the Human Foundation can you create a strong business upon it.

A strong Human Foundation shortcuts conflicts and ensures more of a common ground for your business by:

- Getting to know yourself and your potential (or current) partner incredibly well
- Spotting potential conflicts before they arise

- Setting the ground rules to handle issues prior to partnership
- Perhaps deciding not to go into partnership at all

The bottom line is, building a Human Foundation by using the Partnersh*t-to-Par+nership Process can make all the difference for your business. See what happened with a few of my clients.

7

THE PARTNERSH*T-TO-PAR1NERSHIP
PROCESS IN ACTION

By the time a partnership dissolves, it has dissolved.
—John Updike

I met Kevin Menendez[1] when I was brought in by his client, an emerging hotel group, to create their brand strategy. I must have made an impression, because a year later Kevin called me. He loved the work that I had done with the hotel group, and thought perhaps I could do the same thing for an offshoot of his existing creative business he was thinking of starting with his husband Karl.

Kevin and Karl had been together for ten years, sharing a loft that also served as a production office and locale for photo shoots. Kevin was the photographer and Karl set the appointments, did the books, and in general handled a lot of the business side of things. Now they wanted to build a second business around creating interactive products, and wanted to make sure it was the right step for them as partners, both personally and professionally.

I was excited to try my new process out on them. After all, they had

---

1   While all examples are drawn from real interactions with real people, their names have been changed to ensure their privacy.

an advantage in that they had already built a strong Human Foundation as a couple.

Or had they?

I told them we would need to sit down together for several sessions, in which I would ask them to respond to a series of questions individually. They would answer the questions in writing—no talking—and would need to be completely honest and answer every question as best they could, even if the questions didn't necessarily seem to apply to them or to business. Then each partner would share his answers one by one.

I let them know that there were no right or wrong answers in this process and then set two simple ground rules: First, when one person was speaking, the other person had to pay close attention and just listen to what was being said. He couldn't interrupt, he couldn't add anything, deny anything or disagree with anything—he simply had to listen.

(It's amazing how seldom any of us really listen to each other. When you listen, you're forced to slow down and observe what's going on with the other person. If you can stop listening to that little internal voice that's always commenting and judging and occupying most of the space in your brain and instead *really* pay attention to the other person, how much more do you think you'd learn about them and yourself?)

Second, once each partner had shared his answers, we would then discuss them. I, as the facilitator, would guide the process and look for areas of compatibility and conflict.

You wouldn't think that simply answering a series of questions would bring up so much—but it did. It had to. Kevin is a very type-A personality, and as soon as Karl started sharing, Kevin wanted to interrupt and insert his opinion. I had to constantly remind Kevin to just listen to Karl, who is the quieter, more internally focused partner. Getting them to stay on track was difficult. We'd be working on one set of questions and

Kevin would jump in, saying, "Well what about X?" This was constant. Finally I had to say, "Ok, stop! We're going to be discussing that aspect of partnership later, and you'll see why it's later at that point. Trust the process and just listen."

As the facilitator, I'm not only looking for clues in the actual content of people's answers, but I'm also reading body language and energy between the partners. My job is not to judge people or to tell anyone they're right or wrong. I simply (a) give people the safety and tools to reveal themselves by asking good questions; (b) connect the dots between potential areas of conflict and commonality; and then (c) help them either build a partnership that will be enjoyable and lasting or help them say goodbye and move on. At the very least, most people meet themselves at a deep level for the very first time.

Within the first day, it was pretty clear that energetically these two men were butting heads. I realized they must have been butting heads in their personal lives, too, since we are who we are, whether at home or in the office. Like Tony Robbins says, "How you do one thing is how you do everything." While being life partners comes with a different set of parameters, people are who they are. The business combination of Kevin's enthusiasm and expectations and Karl's steadiness and quieter nature was clearly going to be a challenge.

Notice I said "challenge." Challenges are not bullets to the heart; they are areas of potential conflict but can also be areas of massive creativity. You just need to identify them and recognize their worth—that's a key part of the P²P Process.

More than six months later, both Kevin and Karl told me that not only had the P²P Process clarified the questions they had about partnering in this new business, but it also helped them understand certain problems they had been having in their personal relationship. And they had stopped seeing their relationship counselor. Can you imagine? They had been seeing the counselor for years for the very problems we brought to light in the P²P Process, but the counselor had never asked them these simple questions. I understand that discussing yourself in the context of business is "safer" than having personal-relationship conversations, but in the end, it shouldn't matter how you get there. What matters is the result.

Predictably, the friction in their personal lives had been crossing over into the business side of what they were already doing together because they were very different people when it came to their outlook, dreams, hopes and wishes for business and life.

That's fine—in fact, our differences are what make partnerships and relationships interesting and dynamic. However, you must be aware of what those differences are and *what motivates them*. Motivation is everything, and by the time you go through the process, your motivation and that of your potential partner(s) becomes clear because you have become self-aware.

Bottom line, at the end of the process, Karl (the quieter partner) realized that he didn't want to work in the new business with Kevin. More important, because of the process, Karl was able to finally articulate exactly why he didn't want to be in the business and what exactly he did want. And Kevin had learned to listen.

It was a revelation for them both. The sessions we had greatly improved their marriage and also prevented them from spending years unhappily together in a business venture that one of them didn't want. Kevin and Karl actually took the notes from our session, created a graphic and posted it on the wall of their studio. They tell me that looking at their Partnership Plan (see Appendix A, Ex. A2, Fig A3) keeps them grounded and clear on what's important to them both. Two years later, it's still there. They live by it. And nope—they have not gone back to the counselor.

The sessions benefited Kevin professionally as well, because he was now able to clearly see the patterns he had been running in his life and business that created immense stress and challenge. He also got extremely clear on what he wanted and needed to look for, should he choose to find someone else to partner with professionally. In fact, only a few months later, Kevin called to ask me to run the process again, this time with a gentleman he was thinking of hiring as a CFO and another two men who might possibly become partners.

Was I excited? You'd better believe it. I had learned a lot from the first go-round, and had made significant changes to the process. The group went through the new and improved Partnersh*t-to-Par+nership Process 2.0, and it was clear to everyone, right from the start, that one of the partners simply wasn't going to work out. The process saved them all years of headaches and heartache.

This isn't magic. Wait—maybe it is. There is magic in talking and listening. That's where life is lived.

HELP ME RHONDA

Next up were two female psychologists—one, an on-hiatus wife and mother with a law and psychology degree; and the other, a hardworking, Ph.D.-carrying psychologist/sex therapist who was also a nurse practitioner and businesswoman who had run a major local business for years. Rhonda and Karen had met socially, and their common fields brought them together. Rhonda had the academic, clinical and business background. Karen was an attorney with a master's degree in mental health counseling. She was fashionable, blazingly intelligent, a social force and, we came to find out, a perpetual student.

They called me to help brand their new company. However, since I developed this work, I had established a New Biz Rule (thanks, Bill Maher): I will not strategize or brand a partner-biz until I run the principals through some version of the P²P process. To start with branding is to start in the middle, and I won't go there anymore. I just cannot, in good faith, sit in a room where potential failure might become abundantly clear to me and take people's money.

Karen was a half-hour late for our first and second meetings. I wondered if Rhonda was listening to this clue. While tardiness is not important to everyone, most often it has nothing to do with being late. In my experience, tardiness will ultimately be a dealbreaker because it's directly related to insecurity.

The girls had many compatible areas but when it came to why they were going into business and what each of them expected from the business, the divide was massive. Right off the bat, in the first set of questions, I knew that this was not to be. The value in continuing was for *them* to learn why. They were not seeing it just yet. So we moved ahead.

Rhonda had a practical, tangible view of where this new company was headed, complete with rock-solid ideas for products, books and services. She had a strong business background and was fully committed to making this new enterprise successful and profitable. Karen's was more of a pro bono mentality. Helping people was what motivated her. Also, she felt insecure about her abilities and credentials, especially as they related to Rhonda, and thought perhaps she might need to go back and earn a Ph.D. to play in this particular sandbox. It was clear that Karen found validation in academics, so because of that she minimized the value of her massive charm, innate ability to network and uniquely fashionable creativity.

On the surface, this looked like it should be a match, because each had what the other needed. But Karen's deep insecurity about her academic qualifications ran her life. And from that came her tendency to be late, which I believe is code for insecure. She simply didn't believe in herself. Perhaps she had never taken a deep look.

The outcome was that each lady went her own way, and both are pursuing what makes them happy. And they remain friends. One of the beautiful things about the P²P Process is how useful it is for people to learn valuable things about themselves in a safe, judgment-free environment.

DENISE

Just like way too many people get married again and again because they keep repeating the same stupid mistakes, a lot of folks do the same in business relationships. Like Denise, one of my most recent clients. Denise is a three-time loser, not in love (as far as I know, but it's possible) but in business partnerships. "I'm just unlucky," she said to me during our first session. "I pick the worst partners! We start out as good friends and then it just all falls apart." With just that much information, I already knew why her partnerships had failed. But it was critical to let her talk and understand it for herself.

We went through some of the P²P questions. As she spoke, I wrote key words on the board so she could see her pattern. "I came from a big **family**, where we all pitched in and helped each other, " she said. "I **need** that **camaraderie** and the **feeling of belonging**. We are all such **good friends!**" Denise went on to her first job as a summer camp counselor, where **teamwork** was the order of the day. Of course, she made **friends** with everyone there. After college, she ended up in finance at a big firm in New York. "There was **no support** for anyone at the firm," she said, " and the **competitive backstabbing** was too much for me. It was **isolating.** I didn't feel any of them were my **friends.**" So Denise decided to open her own firm, and, because she **needs** to be surrounded by friends, she partnered with an old sorority sister.

Within a short time, it became obvious that their friendship wasn't enough to support a business partnership, so they broke up.

I'm sure you see her pattern by now. It happened two more times and would have happened again if she hadn't come to see me to do the work. Note that she came alone, yet the results were just as powerful. She was floored when she finally realized that she was looking for a friend, not a partner. Her *need* for friendship bordered on obsession. She had not asked her partners what they wanted because she ass-umed they wanted what she wanted: a friend. Once she understood that, it changed everything for her.

There are all kinds of dating websites that test compatibility factors to make sure you find the perfect match. We have prenuptial agreements that detail exactly who's responsible for what in a marriage. Anyone with any sense Googles those they're dating and maybe even does a background or credit check to make sure they're not inviting a predator or deadbeat into their lives. We take Myers-Briggs testing to see where our career interests lie. Yet how many of these things do we do to get to know ourselves or to go into business with someone? Little to nothing. We "fall in love" with our business idea or our partner and forget to discover whether we're even remotely compatible in the things that are truly important.

Now you know better.

8

PREPARING FOR THE P²P PROCESS: LET'S GET STARTED

There are only two options regarding commitment. You're either in or out. There's no such thing as a life in-between.

—Pat Riley

A business partnership is like a child, and very often that's how partners behave. Both need structure, nurturing, planning, vision, goals and boundaries (and sometimes diapers). In other words, a good, solid foundation upon which to grow and thrive.

It doesn't matter if your partner is your wife, relative, college friend or someone you ran into at a bar. You still won't know what they feel/think/want unless you ask them.

Warning: You're going to come up with all kinds of excuses not to do this. These are some of my favorites:

- Why rock the boat?

- It'll take too long.

- It's too hard.

- I'm just too busy.

- It's too expensive.

- We'll get to it later.

- I don't have time.

- We don't need this.

- This is stupid.

- I want to do it but my partner doesn't.

- Won't she think I'm nosy?

- We're just starting our business. We need to get the doors open first.

- I'm not so sure I want to know him that well.

It's your funeral—or wedding, depending on your choice of metaphor and how you want this partnership to turn out. I so deeply wish I had done this with my partner. It would have eliminated years of angst, misery, wasted effort and financial and emotional loss, and I would still have my friend.

This process is going to get many potential areas of disagreement out of the way and let you negotiate the specific terms of your relationship while you both are cool, calm and collected—instead of turning viciously on each other in the middle of a crisis, letting the accusations fly and digging yourself deeper and deeper into -sh*t with every word.

WHAT I HAVE LEARNED IS THIS:

RIGHT YOUR -SHIP NOW TO AVOID -SH*T LATER.

WHAT YOU WILL NEED FOR THIS PROCESS

1. A genuine commitment. And I mean genuine. Without it, you might as well close this book and go surfing. And when that wave crashes you into the rocks, you'll have some preparation for how it will feel when partnersh*t does the same.

2. **A neutral space.** Don't do this process in your office or in either partner's home. Give it the respect and focus it deserves. Spread out! Find somewhere quiet and neutral, where you can meet in private. Make it a retreat experience.

3. **A whiteboard or easel pad** where you can stick stuff so both of you can see it. Your facilitator will write down everything you say, big as life, so you can see what you are saying and see potential conflicts. Often we don't even hear ourselves as we drone on.

4. **This book, paper, pens and sticky notes.** You're going to be writing and sharing your answers with each other, and posting some of them on a whiteboard or easel (see above). This will be an absolute vision fest! Enjoy the process.

5. **The P²P Process Workbook or the free, downloadable worksheets** available on the AHF Website (http://www.ahumanfoundation. com/downloads). There are two formats: Question Worksheets and Exercise Worksheets.

6. **A mediator/facilitator/moderator.** You cannot do this process with just the two of you. Bring in someone who isn't invested in either partner "winning" or in the success of the business. Ask a business associate (from another company, not from yours if you are already in business), a minister or counselor—but they must have read this book before they work with you. Or, you can contact my office to schedule time with a trained facilitator (info@humanfoundation.com). You will need someone neutral to deeply listen to what both of you are saying, decipher it to find your truths, and then chart the answers on a whiteboard to help you arrive at conclusions.

7. **Time.** Business is serious, and so is this process. Remember, everything is a process, and things take the time they take. So take the time to set things up the right way. You will need to commit to three sessions of four to six hours each for just the first five steps of the P²P Process. The last two steps, Construction and Creation, help you set up the structure, branding and marketing of your business. All seven steps together deliver a complete partnership and business setup. The average time this Process takes is 4 days. If this sounds like a long time, remember: this P²P Process requires exactly the same time and dedication that building your business will. There are no shortcuts.

Schedule this time so you will not be interrupted. Turn off cell phones; disable the email feature or any other Internet capability on your phone. There is nothing more annoying or distracting than this intrusion. Understand that people will try to use the "I have to take this call" excuse to extricate themselves from discomfort. Don't let it happen. It's a human trait to use distraction as a way of avoiding potentially difficult questions or painful emotions. However, this is the time to deal with exactly that—so you won't be blindsided later.

8. **Permission.** Give yourself and your potential partner permission to be honest and forthcoming. This is not a time to sugarcoat or ask for less than you truly want. I guarantee that some of your answers to the questions will not be pretty. You'll look selfish or petty or demanding or whiny or unreasonable, to yourself and to your partner, and they'll look the same to you. In other words, human. That's okay. In this process, honesty isn't just the best policy—it's the only policy, if you want to discover truly if this partnership is right for you. Better now than a million bucks and a heart attack later.

9. **Healthy, nourishing foods and snacks and lots of H₂0.** You will be exercising your brain and spirit, and this can be taxing. Nothing sugary or junky. You don't need a sugar high and its attendant crash that will make you cranky and tired. You are definitely what you eat.

10. **Good energy.** Here is some food for thought about the massive power of energy from *Quantum Success* author Sandra Ann Taylor:

> *Our personal energy moves outward from us and connects us with others of like resonance, determining both who and what we will attract in life. Each of us is like a little radio station, constantly broadcasting signals about our self and our life. The people and situations that match those signals are the ones who will tune into us and be drawn into our life experience.*

So tune in to a good, strong frequency. To be clear, my partner and I had great energy, and we attracted the good in each other for a very long time—until we stopped nurturing that energy. And boy, did it turn on us. So good, strong energy is key.

THE RULES

1. Think freely and for yourself. Don't try to be "right." That's wrong.

2. Answering these questions is not a verbal exercise but rather an honest portrayal of oneself on paper first.

3. Write your answers down in the Workbook or on the Question Worksheets, which will chart your answers so you can use them later to build your Human Foundation Partnership Plan.

4. Don't talk until the facilitator calls on you. Speaking your answers out loud creates an atmosphere of agreement rather than accuracy, and agreement is the last thing you are looking for.

5.   Be honest. There is no right or wrong in any answer you give.

6.   Be very clear; e.g., "I want this business to net $2 million this year" versus "I want this business to make *lotsa* money." See the difference? With the first you can set specific, measurable goals, while the other creates *lotsa* confusion and ass-umptions. ("Lotsa" means different things to different people. In Kevin and Karl's case, one wanted to eventually net $5 million a year, and the other would have been satisfied with $40k. And they had been together 10 years! You seeing a problem here?)

What you are ultimately looking for is a complementary relationship with mutual goals. You're also looking for the ability to compromise. In the end, quite simply, the partnership either is or it isn't. If it isn't, you're better off knowing up front, saving yourself heartache, money and stress.

Go for it! Enjoy the next seven chapters, which take you through the process. Again, steps 1 thru 5 are intensely human-focused, and the last two help you build and create your business. And at the end of it, the "baby" you call your partner-biz will be ready to be born—healthy, happy, with unlimited potential to take on the world.

Let's get started.

BUILD A HUMAN FOUNDATION FOR YOUR PARTNERSHIP: THE FIRST FIVE P^{2}P CATEGORIES

9

#1: CHARACTERIZATION YOUR HUMAN CHARACTER

Be who you are and say what you feel, because those who mind don't matter and those who matter don't mind.
—Dr. Seuss

Who are you?

In this section, we uncover who you are and what motivates you. This partnership starts with you, so you will talk about your personal goals and desires, thoughts, values, ideals and filters. This creates a baseline of your "why," which is, bar none, the most important thing you must know. Your "why" is your motivation. No motivation? No thanks.

Remember, have the facilitator ask you and your partner each question. Then write down your answer in the Workbook or on the Questions worksheet. Don't share your answers or discuss the process until you've answered every question in this section.

Above all, don't overthink this section. Let these answers come naturally. This is your truth and nobody else's.

QUESTION 1:

Why are you here, doing this process?

QUESTION 2:

What is important about answer #1?

QUESTION 3:

Look at answers 1 and 2. What will having those things do for you?

Look carefully at your answer to #3. *This is your filter.* Keep it in your head as you complete this entire process.

Example 9.1

Someone asked me these same three questions at a seminar, and I was blown away by how quickly the answers identified my focus and created clarity. These were my answers, and they still apply to most everything I do.

Question 1: Why are you here?

Because I am curious.

Question 2: What is important about answer #1?

I love to learn. Who I am is a student.

Question 3: Look at answers 1 and 2. What will having those things do for you?

Students are eternally curious. The best teachers are students first and always, and I want to teach.

Do you see how my focus blasted to the top immediately? I am a perpetual student; my filter is curiosity and I approach everything from that vantage point. I rarely have any preconceived idea of what I will learn and am open to whatever that may be.

Now look at this next example for a completely different approach:

Example 9.2

Question 1: Why are you here?
Because my partner made me do this.

Question 2: What is important about answer #1.

Oops. You have set your own trap. Answer # 1 outed you as unwilling/uninterested/forced and all that goes with it.

Question 3: Look at answers 1 and 2. What will having those things do for you?

Your filter is feeling forced, and you are uninterested and unwilling. What outcome do you think you will have if you approach the process (or anything, for that matter) from here?

If this is you, take a look at other parts of your life. Where else is resistance or disinterest showing up? Hmm, something to think about . . .

QUESTION 4:

What is your intention and what outcome do you wish to achieve by completing this process?

You have to declare what you want this process to produce for you before you can create it, both in intention and outcome.

It's like going to a restaurant: You must tell the waiter your order before they can prepare it. Let's say grilled salmon with broccoli is your *outcome*; your intention is to have a relaxing, delicious dinner at your favorite restaurant with the one you love.

Clarity about the endgame will keep you focused and aligned. Remember the key causes of Partnersh*t outlined in Part 1. They bear repeating here:

(1) Lack of self-awareness

(2) Lack of accountability

(3) Lack of clarity

(4) Lack of defined outcome

(5) Inability to negotiate change because there is no basis for renegotiation

Be specific. Setting an intention and creating an outcome are your first big steps toward self-awareness, accountability and clarity.

QUESTION 5:

Will achieving this intention and outcome satisfy you?

If not, take another look at it. Make sure both are what you want and will satisfy you. Do not settle. Do not look for agreement. Do not try to be nice.

Simply be honest.

Let's go back to the restaurant example: If salmon is your outcome but they just ran out, you could change your outcome ("Ok, I'll have the swordfish") yet maintain your intention of having a beautiful evening. However, if the shift in outcome pisses you off ("What do you mean, you're out of salmon? I came here for salmon!"), then your intention was not correct. Having a beautiful evening was not your intention. Your intention was to have salmon.

There are no rights or wrongs here. Either intention is just fine. By not being honest about it, the situation outed you. This will happen every time. So simply be honest about what you want. Go back to the drawing board and start over. Find the intention and outcome that will make you happy and peaceful.

QUESTION 6:

What side of your brain rules?

Left-Brain, Right-Brain Theory is often over-generalized and over-stated but understanding your zones of comfort and discomfort will help you become aware so you can define where you feel best.

Check all that apply:

a. Left Brain: I am . . .

    i. Logical

    ii. Detail oriented

    iii. Factual

    iv. Responsive to language and words

    v. Past and present oriented

    vi. Into math/science

    vii. Responsive to order or patterns

    viii. Reality based

    ix. Strategic

    x. Practical

    xi. Safe   TOTAL NUMBER OF

b. Right-Brain: I am . . .   _____ LEFT BRAIN TRAITS

i. Emotional

ii. Big-picture oriented

iii. Imaginative

iv. Responsive to symbols and images

v. Present and future oriented

vi. Into philosophy/religion/art/music

vii. Good at spatial perception

viii. Fantasy based

ix. Open to possibility

x. Impetuous

xi. Risk-taking

TOTAL NUMBER OF
_____RIGHT BRAIN TRAITS

The side with the highest number of checks is your dominant side.

Why is the Left/Right thing important? We all have traits from both sides of our brains. However, people are happier when they spend the bulk of their time in areas in which they excel and can find success. If you're not a science brain, for example, you probably should not be working in the lab. Knowing what your "brain traits" are will help you declare and position yourself in the areas in which you can succeed. Everyone benefits.

On a partnership level, it's good to be somewhat opposite here, but not mandatory. My partner and I were both dominant right brain, and we soon came to understand there was a big hole in the operation of our business. Remember when I talked earlier about needing a CEO? Had we identified this need earlier, the partnership and our business would have been better for it.

What's your preferred style of relating?

☐ **Are you an Introvert?**

> More inward focused; more occupied with thinking/feeling; minimizes contact with people; uncomfortable around unknown people

☐ **Are you an Extrovert?**

> Outward focused; more occupied with doing/action; loves to be around other people; empowered in social situations

☐ **Are you an Ambivert?**

> Strong characteristics of both

If your thing is intricate computer programming and you find yourself in a state of complete and utter joy locked away for days in a quiet room, your partner probably wouldn't be wise in assuming you'll be the business rainmaker. Conversely, if you're the one who's first to the party and lives for the next opportunity to talk to people about your business, your partner had better not expect you to spend your weekends going through the books line by line.

What is your approach to getting things done?

☐ **Ready. Aim. Fire.**

☐ **Ready. Fire. Aim.**

You are what you are. Best to be aware of it. Cartoon character Quick Draw McGraw was a classic Ready.Fire.Aim., but he had Baba Looey at his side to at least warn him about the trouble his trigger-happiness was about to cause. Of course, Quick Draw rarely listened. Moral of the story? Watch out for those Quick Draws. They rarely think before they act, and more often than not this will spell big trouble.

Here's a nightmare scenario: two Quick Draws. Yikes. Someone in your partnership has to be the voice of reason.

Would you describe your personality/drive (NOT your sexual identity) as dominant masculine or dominant feminine?

No, this question is not about who you are sleeping with or what team you play for. It's about the transfer of human energy.

While we're either male or female in gender, each of us has a dominant personality that we show the world. Remember Linda Hamilton in *Terminator*? No doubt she's a woman. But her *energy* was totally masculine and she'd kick your butt at the least provocation.

Film writer Adam Karabel calls this trait *feminine masculinity*: women who step into roles (movie or societal) traditionally played by men.

Perhaps the most popular example of this role-reversal is Angelina Jolie and Brad Pitt in *Mr. and Mrs. Smith*. No doubt he's a hunk and she's a babe. But when it comes to *cojones*, hers rule.

Mine did too, until they didn't. I was dominant masculine in my business and most things most of my life, until the partnership fell apart. That trauma changed everything. I made an almost-instantaneous transformation to the feminine, which,

I discovered, is who I really am once the guard comes down. Realizing my true nature was quite potent. I like it better in my natural feminine state. I feel like I am home.

Not everyone shifts, and not everyone has to or should shift. Just be aware and comfortable that the energy you are putting out there is healthy and working.

I'm sure strong fems and burly machos end up as partners all the time, but likely they ultimately blow each other up. Evidence shows me there is a balance in the really great partnerships.

I am . . .

☐ **Dominant masculine**

> Physical, strong, centered, purposeful, directed, on a mission, problem solver, competitive, ownership, word-driven, able to cut the cord

☐ **Dominant feminine**

> Nurturing, emotional, sensation-based, loving, open, unable to cut the cord

Does your partner agree with your assessment?

News flash: People might not see you the way you see yourself. If there were ever a time to ask this question, it's now. Be sure to listen to the answer. It's not yours to like; it's yours to listen to and learn from. And again, there are no right or wrong answers. There is just the answer.

Are you...

☐ Batman?

☐ Robin?

Here a quiz: How many bosses can there be?

Repeat after me: ONE.

Knowing, understanding, accepting and being at peace with this is going to be at the heart of your ability to be a good partner. If a power struggle ensues, your chances for partnership success aren't great. Like probably zero.

What feeds you? (accomplishment, giving, travel, money, possessions, people, learning, etc.)

Partners need to know what motivates the other. This can be as simple as someone who needs high praise to spur them on. If you know this about your partner, a simple "Great job, buddy" now and then can avert a zillion potential problems. Or if your partner is a contribution junkie, then by all means it will be important to include pro bono accounts into the client mix.

What limits you? (fear, laziness, lack of focus, unavailability, obligation, etc.)

If you are scared to death, now's the time to talk about it. When in your life can you admit what everyone else can see in you anyway, in a safe environment, and potentially slay that dragon forever? People can see who we are even though we try to hide our dark side. So let it out into the sunshine where it won't cause unexpected trouble. If laziness is your thing, your partner needs to know and you need to schedule lazy time into your schedule. If you're an insomniac, let someone know so they can cover for you when needed. If what limits you is an illness or caring for a sick parent, tell your partner so you can work around it.

QUESTION 13:

What makes you angry?

Everyone has a trigger, so just 'fess up. Mine is hearing people complain. For me, that is nails-on-the-chalkboard time. I also draw a very hard line when it comes to people being unprepared for meetings or presentations. What ticks you off? Say it. Then nobody can say they weren't warned.

QUESTION 14:

What is your best quality?

QUESTION 15:

What is your greatest strength?

Yes, the whole world might already know these things about you, but there is power in declaring this out loud. Yours can be a bright personality, with patience, acceptance or whatever sun shines on you. You may possess a Herculean amount of energy. Any great quality and strength is also a business/partnership asset. Use these to everyone's benefit.

QUESTION 16:

What is your absolute worst quality?

QUESTION 17:

What is your greatest weakness?

Like those above, these two are not the same question. I'll use me as the example. My worst *quality* is my temper. My greatest *weakness* is my complete inability to function unless I have had lots and lots of sleep. (Of course, when I've had too little sleep, my temper flares. It's a circle.) Anyone who works with me has to know these things.

QUESTION 18:

What will you absolutely not tolerate under any circumstances?

Say it loud and proud. One of my clients hates smoking. With a passion bordering on psychotic. She chooses not to date, partner or even work with someone who smokes. Another client cannot tolerate noise. Yet another goes off when people are texting during meetings. I have seen him leave the room. Another hates to be corrected. Whatever it is, once you say it, there's more room where it is (out in the world) than where it was (stuck in your gut and making you angry, sick or both).

QUESTION 19:

What do you absolutely refuse to do?

When I started my RFP/Business Plan business, I had to learn Quick-Books to keep track of the business bookkeeping. I can tell you that I would rather eat raw lizard than have anything to do with the accounting side of running a business. While I have many left-brain tendencies, numbers aren't one of them. That is not to say I can't read a P/L statement, because I can, and every business owner/partner needs to learn this skill. However, I cannot nor will I ever attempt to prepare one. Remember Valerie, the CFO who came in and saved my sanity when my business was going down the drain? That's why God made her. I let her do her job.

QUESTION 20:

List the 10 most important things/emotions/ areas that you value in your life.

Values are inherent in building a Human Foundation. After all, what are we but who and what we love and value? My writing partner Vicki points out that you might interpret this question as in "I value my '65 Chevy Camaro." That's not necessarily what we are looking for here. However, once you dig deeper, you might uncover that what you really value is nostalgia or style. These are just some examples of values; perhaps they will inspire your creative process.

Example 9.3

Love	Clarity
Health	Contribution
Success	Curiosity
Financial freedom	Cheerfulness
Adventure	Flexibility
Accountability	Determination
Family/friendship	Inspiration
Honesty	Confidence
Integrity	Faith
Passion	Spirituality
Fun	Joy
Respect	Gratitude
Profitability	Education

Partners and businesses must develop and operate from core values. They are the rules of the road and will pop up again in the Brand Strategy segment of creating a business. See Section See Section B, Chapter 16, #7. Core values come from both sides of the partnership table. The *best* businesses make these hugely important and live within them. By declaring your personal values now, you're also setting the stage for creating your company's brand strategy later. And if you end up a solo practitioner? Values are still bedrock. Declare them. Write them down. Live by them.

Example 9.4

My favorite core values example comes from one of my favorite companies: Zappos. They live by their very simple, customer-centric mission statement ("To provide the best customer service possible") and express that every day by *Delivering Happiness* (also the title of CEO Tony Hsieh's bestseller about his entrepreneurial efforts and the Zappos culture).

My team and I had the good fortune to visit their headquarters in Las Vegas and hear Hseih speak. What they stand for has nothing to do with what they sell. It's always and only about *people*. In my book (figuratively and literally), this sets them apart.

Their core values are prominently displayed on their office walls, lest anyone forget. And they don't, because their culture is empowered, collegial and service-oriented.

1) Deliver WOW Through Service
2) Embrace and Drive Change
3) Create Fun and A Little Weirdness
4) Be Adventurous, Creative and Open-Minded
5) Pursue Growth and Learning
6) Build Open and Honest Relationships With Communication
7) Build a Positive Team and Family Spirit
8) Do More With Less
9) Be Passionate and Determined
10) Be Humble

This is the best example of clarity of mission that I have ever seen. More on mission later.

Example 9.5

April Norris (april-norris.com) is a healer, in every sense of the word. I helped her get clear about how to run her business, what her products are and what she stands for. I love what she did with her core values. This artwork exemplifies April, and she lives by everything on this tree.

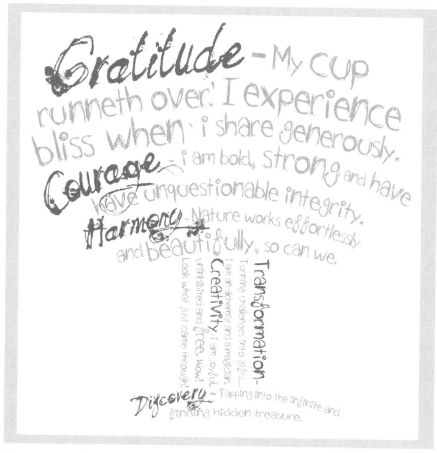

Figure 9.1 *April Norris core values.*

Example 9.6

My Core Values

Over time, I have watched my core values evolve with my emotional growth. You can probably guess as to what is important to me simply by reading this book.

What I Live By:

Health and Wellness.
My body, mind and spirit are nourished with good food, good habits and good decisions.

Ready. Aim. Fire.
Thought before action.
I am not for everybody,
and everybody is not for me.

Honor.
There is that moment when your heart feels full;
when you stand taller; your head is lifted
and eyes look toward the sky.
Honor is a state, not a word.
You feel it, and those around you feel it too.

Gratitude.
I'm grateful for all that I am
and all whom I have in my life.

Alignment.
Everything is in perfect harmony
and as it should be.
I am aware and accountable.

Figure 9.2   *Patty Soffer core values.*

Where and how do you get energy? Will this business/ partnership feed or support that?

Are you like Bill Clinton, where you suck energy from the crowds around you, or are you more like Hillary, who, according to her *Elle* magazine profile (April 2012), is more an introvert and feels drained by crowds? Do you need constant physical activity to stay happy, or are you okay sitting in front of your iMac? If you need to be surrounded by people, noise, general chaos and a spirit of *joie de vivre* and that is anathema to your potential partner, you will run into issues. You must be aware of any conflict and work to create harmony.

In the spirit of "Baby Shoes" by Ernest Hemingway, write a captivating tale of who you are in exactly six words.

Legend has it that Ernest Hemingway created the shortest short story ever told while having lunch at New York City's famous Algonquin Hotel Round Table writers hangout. He bragged that he could write a captivating tale—complete with beginning, middle, and end—in only six words. A bar bet ensued; Hemingway quickly scribbled six words down on a napkin and passed it around. As each writer read the napkin, they conceded he'd won.

Those six words?

"For sale. Baby shoes. Never worn."

This is an example of something called "flash fiction." I have tailored it for this process and am calling it a "flash bio." When you have only 6 words to tell your story, you will dig deeply and find the right words.

Over time, this has bar none become the favorite question in all of the process. Remember Kevin and Karl? Here are Karl's (the quiet one) six words:

Grew up alone. With someone forever.

Do you understand now why he's so quiet? And loyal? Kevin damn near fell off his chair. He'd never understood Karl in that simple way. It was an emotional moment—a huge shift for them both. Which leads to the next question . . .

QUESTION 23:

Do you think your partner sees you this way?

If not, you will have some deep conversations ahead. Now is the time. The Process will help clarify any doubts either of you might have.

QUESTION 24:

What are you grateful for?

Really, have you ever stopped to ask yourself this very important question?

I'm big on gratitude, as you can see by now. I am grateful for my eyes. My heart. My family. My life. A new day. Flowers. My health. My brain. Can you see how this might change your outlook? Being aware of and in a state of gratitude is a huge life, partnership and business asset.

I love it when people think this is a woo-woo question. Quite the opposite. It is perhaps the most human question one could ask. This is the exact question you need to ask yourself when the sh*t starts to hit the fan-—and it will. To focus on what you are grateful for will mitigate whatever problem you are facing.

What are we looking for in this section?

YOUR SELF-AWARENESS

- Who you are
- Your predispositions
- Your self-image
- Your motivation
- Your passion
- Your pain points
- Your level of candor
- The prism/filter through which you experience the world

People high in self-awareness are remarkably clear in their understanding of what they do well, what motivates and satisfies them, and which people and situations push their buttons.

—Travis Bradberry, co-author of Emotional Intelligence 2.0

I hope you and your partner have discovered much that will help you determine both your inner workings and the way you might work together. The level of honesty you both bring to the process will make all the difference in its long-term effectiveness.

That honesty is about to be tested! Because the next step is to share what you just wrote down with the other person. Here's how to share without getting mired in sh*t:

Rules Reminder:

1. The facilitator asks one question at a time.

2. Each partner reads his or her answers, uninterrupted. No comments or editorializing from anyone!

3. The facilitator writes the answers on the easel or whiteboard.

Exercise

After both partners have answered all the questions in this section and listened to your partner's answers, list the areas of compatibility, conflict and compromise in your partnership and how you will address them. Use your Workbook or as many downloaded Exercise Worksheets as necessary.

Example 9.7

One potential partnership group I worked with consisted of four people, all spouses of each other.

Couple #1, Sharon and Alberto, had been together on and off for nearly a decade, and it had been a rocky road, to be sure. The personality conflicts were substantial. Alberto had recently lost his job at a huge multinational conglomerate, so for the first time was testing the entrepreneurial waters. Additionally, it was also his first crack at not being the breadwinner. He was on new turf.

The potential business concept we were exploring was Sharon's idea. In other words, there was a new sheriff in town, and she was ready to wear the badge.

Add to the mix another couple, Peter and Isaac, who also had been together for many years but were self-aware, comfortable in their roles, already successful in their own right and peaceful. They were more than a little bit wary about the potential ruts and valleys a partnership like this would introduce into their lives.

The group had recently met via Sharon, and the attraction of becoming partners had everything to do with the type of business they were going into. A business that married the beauty industry with the self-help industry, it had components that appealed to everyone concerned. But you already know that this is not enough for a solid partnership foundation. You need compatibility in many more areas than just that.

We uncovered a few compatibilities and several areas of conflict in this first section:

	WHAT FEEDS YOU?	WHAT LIMITS YOU?	WHAT WON'T YOU TOLERATE?
SHARON	Helping Connecting Pride Accomplishment	*Not sleeping* *My grumpiness*	Words that don't match actions
ISAAC	$$$ Continuity; like things to be the consistent *Dogs* *Peter being happy*	Fear of the unknown	Tardiness *When people don't listen*
ALBERTO	Accomplishment Growth Family	Lack of clarity = anger = I quit! *Bad temper*	Disrespect *Challenging my intelligence*
PETER	Love *Giving* People Change Growth *Laughter* Big picture/being able to see the vision Creativity Photography	My tardiness Taking on too much Talking too much *I get scattered*	Abuse

Figure 9.3 *The items in italics are areas of conflict.*

You would think that laughter, dogs and Peter would be peaceful areas, but when you look at grumpiness, not sleeping, anger, temper etc., you can see this behavior will mitigate any laughter Peter might have, and once Peter becomes unhappy, Isaac is too. See below:

CONFLICTS	IMPACT	COMPROMISE
Personality Conflicts Sharon is tightly wound. Alberto has a short temper/ is impatient, which spins her out. It creates a cycle that leads to stress, sleeplessness and then back to temper. This dynamic will be as present in the partnership as it currently is in private life. It must be managed or it will wreak havoc with everyone.	Peter and Isaac will feel the stress from Sharon and Alberto's relationship. While some relationships thrive on stress, keep in mind that there are four people in this potential partnership. Isaac in particular will not thrive in this environment. He fears the unknown. Peter is generally a happy person and all the things that feed him will be dampened by the infighting.	**Product Opportunity** Develop a system for managing disagreements/stress. Then market this system to teach others (revenue opportunity). Use your own experiences as examples to your clients. When you become the example that has triumphed over adversity, people listen. It gives you credibility.

Figure 9.4 *Conflict, impact and compromise*

Because of the self-help nature of the business they are building, I acted as both facilitator and brand strategist, and looked for product opportunities in both the areas of conflict and compatibility. Often, conflict teaches our best lessons and opens a space for something new. In this case, they are working to develop a stress management program and position it as a profit center.

Next, we looked at who wants to be the boss and where that drive comes from.

	READY/AIM/FIRE?	BATMAN/ROBIN?	DOMINANT MASCULINE/ FEMININE?	LEFT BRAIN/ RIGHT BRAIN?
SHARON	RAF	*Batman*	Feminine	Right
ISAAC	RAF	Robin	Masculine	Right
ALBERTO	RAF	*Batman*	Feminine	Left
PETER	*RFA*	*Batman*	Masculine	Left
	COMPATIBILITY	*CONFLICT*	COMPATIBILITY	COMPATIBILITY

Figure 9.5   *Who's the boss? Areas of conflict are in italics*

Three people wanting to be the boss is a tough one to get around. Often, when conflict arises in other categories, there are other traits and circumstances that will mitigate some of the conflict. Not so here. It's pretty basic: there can only be one boss.

CONFLICTS	IMPACT	COMPROMISES
High potential for a power struggle We determined that there are three Batmans (Batmen?) and one Robin in this potential partnership.	**High potential for infighting**	Be clear and accepting about who the true Batman is. Batman must empower the team.

Figure 9.6 *Conflicts, impact and compromises.*

Ultimately, this group became a two-person strategic partnership. Peter and Isaac dropped out, and the remaining two are working together on a per project basis. To date, they have not formed a formal partnership and probably will not. We determined that there is no great reason for them to partner. They can buy each other's time as needed.

10

#2: COLLABORATION
WORKING TOGETHER
TO ACHIEVE A SHARED GOAL

The secret is to gang up on the problem, rather than each other.
—Thomas Stallkamp

You. Me. Us.

In this section, we uncover how you approach partnership and business and how both will fit into your life. We define your skills, strengths and weaknesses, what you expect from a partner and what you are willing to give. Don't be polite. Be honest.

QUESTION 1:

Define "partnership."

Is your definition compatible with that of your partner?

Like someone defining "relationship" or "marriage," you may be surprised to learn that your definition is completely at odds with your prospective partner. And wouldn't THAT be fun—to be harnessed together while pulling in opposite directions?

Why do you want a partner?

This is the time to spill your guts. If you want this because you're scared or broke or need your green card, your potential partner needs to know. If that is the case, don't stop here. Once it's on the table and you complete the rest of the process, there might be other circumstances that show you there is no reason to be scared (or that the green card won't be a problem). You will definitely find your voice in this process—and one of the most essential things in a partnership is to be able to speak your truth even when it's not pretty.

Is there another way you could work together without being partners?

A lot of people move straight to partner without considering their other options. That's kind of like going out on dates with everyone you meet and assuming that marriage must be the final outcome. That attitude puts a lot of pressure on the dates and can cause you to ignore a lot of very important warning signs.

Partnership is a big deal—mentally, emotionally, financially, legally and every other-ly. Even though you may think your potential partner is the greatest prophet since Moses, if you're not significantly compatible the chances of partnersh*t are high. That doesn't mean you still can't create a business relationship that benefits you both. You could form an alliance between two separate businesses, or one of you could hire the other as an independent contractor or supplier. This question should help you think outside of the partnership track and perhaps lead to a much more enjoyable kind of relationship for you both.

QUESTION 5:

What are the most important qualities are you looking for in a partner? (honesty, skill, financial strength, etc.)

For this question and all others for that matter, word choice is important and specific. I believe there are no synonyms. A thing means what it means: "knowledgeable" and "brilliant" do not mean the same thing; neither do "powerful" and "controlling," though the dictionary says they are synonyms. So be careful to use the exact words you mean.

You might say you're looking for a supportive person to partner with, but what does this really mean? Is it okay that your potential partner might support you like steel beams support a high rise, but flits around like Marilyn Monroe, flirting with the men and making the women in the office uncomfortable, not to mention opening you up to harassment lawsuits? This behavior undermines the very fabric of a company and makes you look bad. That's not being supportive. That's being selectively supportive—not at all the same and not acceptable.

Define, down to the last word, what these qualities are. Then settle for nothing less.

QUESTION 6:

Describe the perfect day in your life.

QUESTION 7:

Will this partnership and business feed that?

If your perfect day is sitting on the beach in solitude and your partner and/or business requires you to spend all of your time on the phone or in person drumming up business, you're probably not going to be happy. Conversely, if you're a people person and the business is software development and managing back-end services that have been outsourced to India, you're not going to get enough "face time" with others to scratch your social itch.

Yes, partners need to have complementary styles and strengths, but you'd better make sure that somewhere along the way your needs are being met by both the business and your partner. You can take a look at your answers to Question 19 in the last chapter to give you an idea about what you need in a partnership.

How do you envision your lifestyle as a result of this partnership/ business?

Is it substantially different from what it is now? How?

These two questions address your expectations around the partnership and the business. Answering them will help you gain clarity in two ways. First, if your expectations are dramatically different from your partner's—you expect the business to get you into the *Lifestyles of the Rich and Famous* category, while your partner is looking to produce a little extra income to put the kids through college—you may find yourself fighting about how much risk to take on, how hard each of you has to work, whether to expand quickly or slowly and so on.

Second, your expectations may be completely out of line with the potential of the business and even your real desires. You may love the idea of a big house and a huge pool and a private jet parked at the local airport, but (1) your little carpet-cleaning business may not ever support that kind of lifestyle, or (2) you may be caught up in the dream of being rich without understanding the tradeoffs.

Now, I'm not one to shoot down anybody's dreams—far from it. Dreams are the only things that carry most businesses in the beginning. But it's important to be clear—and realistic—about exactly how your business and this partnership will affect your life and your lifestyle, right from the start.

So speak up, because unfulfilled expectations will cause trouble.

Once declarations appear, expectations disappear, and you are on much safer ground.

What does a typical workday look like to you? Define specifically.

Is it important that your partner has the same definition?

These questions aren't designed to make you believe that every day is a golf day or that you're not getting anything done unless you put in 96 hours a week. Small businesses are susceptible to extremes. Understand how important it is to design a partnership and a business that fits your needs and wants, so you will want to want to work and will work smart.

Lisa Cherney, author of *Inspiration to Realization,* ultimately wanted to be with her children as often as possible. She said, " I took many steps to expand my business and ultimately triple my income, and one of these steps was affirming this three-days-a-week work lifestyle. Think about your life and your business. Affirm and explore and decide on what lifestyle you want to have while balancing everything there is to balance."

Hers is a very specific lifestyle/workstyle desire with a very specific solution. You need to partner with someone who can accept you the way you are. By designing the partnership and business right out of the gate, as opposed to letting it design you, there is no room for those deadly ass-umptions that people make about each other.

What are you good or great at, both tangible and intangible? (e.g., typing, negotiation, bookkeeping, schmoozing, etc.)

Brag on yourself—this is no time to be shy—but also be honest. Don't say you're a super bookkeeper if the extent of your experience is balancing your personal checkbook. At the same time, if you oversaw all the volunteers for the last PBS fundraising campaign, you're probably a pretty good manager even if you've never done something like that in your own business. Skills are transferable, so think carefully on this one. Make sure you assess your skills and strengths as clearly and as comprehensively as possible.

What are you bad at, both tangible and intangible?

This is the time to state loudly and proudly what you don't do well and what you hate doing. You suck at paperwork? Put it down! You wouldn't be caught dead making outbound sales calls? Say so with gusto! Be clear so you don't get stuck running the IT department if your talents run toward marketing.

What specific skills and talents will our business need?

This list will depend on the business you are in or are looking to start. Some skills are basic: accounting, sales, managing. Other skills are business specific— creative abilities, computer programming/ software development training, construction or plumbing skills, manufacturing expertise, etc. Again, make this list as clear and as comprehensive as you can. It'll help you figure out which partner does what, and who else you may need to hire to fill in the gaps.

What skills and talents are missing from this partnership?

When it comes to the fundamental skills of running a business, several years ago I learned that people are either Entrepreneurs, Managers or Producers. The *Entrepreneur* is the visionary who attracts talent, takes all the risk and is a big-picture person. You should leave the details to the *Managers*, who like to run the day-to-day operations of a business. The third category, *Producers*, are out there creating, inventing, selling, innovating and influencing.

We are all at our best in only one of these areas. The "I-can-multi-task" person might have several perceived talents, but most likely his or her degree is in "Busy Administration," which is a form of control that will eventually cause gridlock and other problems. So nail down the specific, marketable skills that you have and that your partnership/business must have to operate successfully. And then go buy what you don't have.

What will your title be?

Do your skills, talents and strengths live up to your title?

Job titles are usually a sensitive area in any partnership because they're closely tied to ego. More than that, your job title will communicate your position, level of responsibility and the skills and abilities you bring to the business. If your title is CFO, you'd better be good with numbers; a "Managing Partner" had better be happy handling all the day-to-day details. The worst title of all is simply "partner"—unless you are attorneys, and even then I do not recommend it unless you have an accompanying job description.

Understand that these don't have to be the titles you use on your business card: there, you can go crazy and call yourself anything you want. My entrepreneurial friend Jessica signs off as The Chief and David, a logistics expert, calls himself the Force Multiplier. Whether you're Queenbee, Vulcan Ruler, Dr. Feelgood or Deputy Dog, be very clear about what you are and what you do.

Write your job description. Be very detailed and clear.

This question alone will save you years of frustration, especially once you and your partner compare job descriptions and agree on them.

What scares or concerns you about your partner or this partnership? Why?

What excites you about your partner or this partnership? Why?

Emotions are going to be part of any business and any partnership. Better to get them out in the open now, so you can make an effort to handle anything that scares or concerns you and your partner, and increase the factors that excite you both.

What do you expect from your partner(s)?

What can your partner(s) expect from you?

What expectations do you have of yourself?

Ahhh, expectations… they're like mines underneath that beautiful meadow called "your partnership." You can't see them, yet as soon as you trip over one there's bound to be an explosion and lots of carnage.

For example, Jackie and Matt are both long-established, prominent interior designers, and are new partners thanks to the merger of their individual companies into one successful, high profile firm. Things were going smoothly, except for one thorny issue. Matt is a morning person, therefore expecting everyone else to be as well. However, Jackie is a night owl who does most of her creating in the wee hours, so often she does not arrive at the office until the afternoon, which is what she has done for years as a solo practitioner. Matt interpreted this as slacking off, and one day when he could no longer stifle his frustration, their land mine exploded. It didn't end the partnership, but it caused trouble and hurt feelings that took time to subside. Only after we did the P²P Process, did Matt finally understand that even though Jackie was wired differently than he was, her work contribution was stellar. And she was not going to change her ways to satisfy him.

The only way to avoid these expectation land mines is to bring them out into the open. Do not ass-ume anything. Verbalizing your expectations will help you know exactly what's important to you and help you both to understand why and what to do when those "mines" explode.

What do you like the most about your partner(s)? Why?

This to me is like the gratitude question in the last section. We don't tell people often enough why we like them and what they do is great. Keep this description handy and pull it out whenever your partner ticks you off. And be prepared, because oddly enough, the thing you most like about this partner will be the very thing that makes you crazy down the road. ("Oh I just love her powerful voice" quickly turns into "Damn it, she sounds like a braying donkey!")

Get down and personal now, or get down and personal later in a lawyer's office. Either way, you *will* get personal. I guarantee it.

QUESTION 25:

Now define Partnership again. Has your definition changed since you started this section?

What Are We Looking for in this Section?

Collaboration is your ability to work with others. I'm sure as you went through this section you learned a lot about yourself, specifically...

YOUR COLLABORATION POTENTIAL

- Your desires
- Your passion
- Your lifestyle
- Your work style
- Your skills
- Your strengths and weaknesses
- Your expectations and fears
- Your ability to self-manage
- Your ambitions
- Your candor

When we act individually, whether with a political motivation, as part of our jobs, or as an artistic endeavor, we are limited by our weaknesses . . . No matter how skilled an individual may be, he or she will still exhibit weaknesses based upon knowledge, strength, political and social pull, etc. By the same token, we all have strengths, and not everyone's strengths are equal to one another. In this way, when banding together, weaknesses are minimized and strengths of all are accentuated.

—Rhonda Levine, Bright Hub

You're about to learn a whole lot more. The real power of this section comes from revealing your answers to your partner and discovering how your answers are compatible—or not. This section alone will save you hundreds of thousands of dollars and years of standing hip deep in partnersh*t, wishing you had never crossed paths with the psycho you thought you knew so well.

Once again, have the facilitator ask each question in order, or have each partner read his or her answer to each question without interruption or comments. Use your Workbook or Question Worksheets to answer. Then he/she will write all the answers on the easel or whiteboard.

Exercise

After both partners have answered all the questions in this section and listened to your partner's answers, list the areas of compatibility, conflict and compromise in your partnership and how you will address them. Use your Workbook or as many downloaded Exercise Worksheets as necessary.

Example 10.1

Andrea and Emily met at a yoga class that Andrea was teaching and soon became friends. Rather quickly, they formed a partnership to open a yoga-based travel business. Like most partners, they had a mutual passion, so after coming up with their spiritual travel concept, off they went to file corporate docs and do the logo/website/brochure tango.

Ironically, their first trip was a raging success in many ways (great location, good events/side trips/food etc.), but there was serious bad blood between Em and some of the clients, who were there to have a spiritual experience and instead found themselves in arguments

	WHY DO YOU WANT TO BE A PARTNER?	WHAT WILL YOUR TITLE BE?	WHAT DO YOU EXPECT FROM YOUR PARTNER?
ANDREA	*I can't do this alone.* *I am afraid to have my own business alone because I don't think I could do it.*	Yoga Master for Inner Wellness	Em's skills are what I am missing. She can run the business while I take care of my clients.
EMILY	I *need* Andres to make this business work. She has all the clients. I don't like working alone *I know Andrea needs me too. She can't do this on her own.*	CEO CFO COO	*I know more about business than Andrea. I think she should let me take care of everything and she should just teach the lessons.*
	Too much need here. Both sides are approaching this business from a point of weakness. Andrea is looking for someone to rescue her from her fear. Em wants to control everything she possibly can.	Em appears to have it all together but her title is based on a need for control, not on what will benefit the company.	Again, the master/victim roles are at work.

Figure 10.1 *Wants, needs likes, fears and expectations. Areas of conflict are in italics.*

with her. This went against everything Andrea stood for.

When Andrea came to me for help, they were already buried in Partnersh*t. They were fighting and very unhappy, even though their business concept was a winner. But there was so much wrong with this pairing that nothing could save it. They have since split and not only are they not partners, but they are no longer friends. The main issue was their absolute inability to collaborate with each other. They came to severe emotional blows and that was the end of that. There was no possibility of repairing this and no point in trying. They were just not compatible. Take a look.

WHAT DO YOU EXPECT FROM YOURSELF?	WHAT DO YOU LIKE MOST ABOUT YOUR PARTNER?	WHAT SCARES YOU ABOUT YOUR PARTNER?
I will bring my clients and design the curriculum.	She's organized. She's strong.	*She's aggresive and bossy. My clients don't like her. She makes me feel like her child. She wants to control everything, especially me.*
I'll take care of the details, handle the money, and make the deals with the hotels/carriers.	Andrea is very soft and sweet. *She's pretty weak and needs* someone strong beside her.	*I am afraid Andrea will leave.*
Money is always an issue and should be under the purview of both partners. It's likely that Em will control this as she does most other things, which is terrible for the partnership.	This is a play on Andrea's perceived weakness and is a play for control.	Because Andrea is a healer, she realizes that what is happening here are childhood fears, both hers and Em's, being reenacted. How interesting that these two found each other!

11

#3: COMMUNICATION SHARING IS IMPORTANT

When someone shows you who they are, believe them the first time.
—Maya Angelou

Your communication style is as important as anything you do. It is the ultimate sharing device; who we are and what we have to give are both our greatest joy and our greatest challenge. Communication is not just verbal and body language but the expression of your very character. It expresses how you operate, interact, treat people, get results, motivate, control, manage stress, provide information and solve problems.

According to research conducted by Optimize International's Steve Lishansky with business professionals in more than 40 countries, they, by their own admission, are effective communicators 60-80% of the time. This might sound good until you realize that it leaves a whopping 20-40% opportunity for miscommunication. It does not take much to wreak havoc under these circumstances. And as mentioned in Part 1, the digital world has opened a Pandora's Box of communication portals and much, like satire, humor, sarcasm and irony (and personal photos), is lost in translation, leaving the door open for out-of-context interpretation and mass distribution that often even the best crisis communication specialist cannot fix. Just ask New York State Representative Anthony Weiner. With little effort and much regret, you can Tweet or email yourself into a nightmare you can't take back or destroy, as the "evidence" lives forever. Think about words like "permanent, searchable and forwarding" before you press "send." Digital info spreads like a wildfire in California and it's hard to regrow what has been destroyed.

QUESTION 1:

What is your communication style? (loud, funny, quiet, electronic, face-to-face, etc.)

QUESTION 2:

What is your personal style? (corporate, hippie, cautious, carefree, etc.)

QUESTION 3:

How do you best express yourself? (writing, singing, speaking, poetry, nonverbal, dance, etc.)

Just because someone is not a chatterbox doesn't mean he/she is not communicating. When my son was in his early teens, a tough time for us all, he had something to tell me that was not easy for him to verbalize. He put a specific Tupac Shakur song in the CD player and I instantly understood what he was trying to say. All these years later, I still remember the impact it had on me and the lesson I learned about communication.

QUESTION 4:

What kind of communication don't you like? (face to face, phone, texting, etc.)

Texting rules the day—or so it seems. However, electronic communication cuts both ways. It's convenient, it's instantaneous, but it's dangerous. Anyone who's had an email misconstrued or worse, been ticked off, vented in either text or email, and then hit the "send" button too quickly knows what I mean.

Remember my Mexico story. Be careful of email. It's a terrible way to communicate depth, meaning and nuance.

QUESTION 5:

What makes you happy?

QUESTION 6:

What shuts you down? (crying, loudness, fighting, etc.)

Remember Tom Hanks' famous line in *A League of their Own*—"There's no crying in baseball"? I have been reminded of that many times as I've analyzed the demise of my partnership. I realize now that being shut out shut me down and made me cry. And I am convinced that my partner couldn't bear to see me in tears. I am absolutely sure neither of us had any idea the buttons we were pushing. If we had, we would have come at each other in a very different, more powerful manner. So be very open about this answer.

What is your dominant mood? (serious, happy, sad, pensive, silly, etc.)

Most people's moods change more frequently than the weather (even here in Miami). But most of us have a "hometown" mood that we come back to. How would you feel if you were a Little Miss Sunshine who went into partnership with Mr. Depresso? By the end of a month, you'd want to kill each other.

Like dominant hands, dominant moods are hard to change. A half-empty-glass person can work with a half-full-glass partner, and in fact there are some benefits in partnering with someone who's not like you. But you'd better be aware of and be willing to put up with the tensions created by your emotional mismatch.

What bothers you? (Noise, tardiness, sloppiness, etc.)

One of my clients told me his business partner was always late—always. It drove him nuts. Of course, to the partner, it didn't matter how late he came into the office as long as he got the work done (at least in the beginning, anyway...).

Everyone has a pet peeve that's his or her own version of fingernails on a blackboard. My client will always hate smoking. Sharon hates noise. Someone else might be driven crazy by elevator music or red ink. The trigger doesn't have to be logical, but if you're smart you'd better communicate what it is.

How do you communicate when you're under stress or in a crisis?

Business equals stress and crises—usually lots of them. If you're a "stomp around the office and throw things" person and that puts your partner under even more stress, you need to talk (and maybe get some counseling). Dump it all on the table now. The secret you try to keep today will be the disaster you will have to manage tomorrow.

How do you release stress?

See the comment above. Throwing things, drinking, overspending, gambling or other bad responses to stress can put a lot of strain on you as well as your partnership. Know your capacity for stress, know when you are hitting overload and create a habit of taking a break when you need it. A look at these patterns now will help you come up with some alternatives that are healthier for you both.

In a crowded room, do you stand out or stand outside?

We're back to the introvert/extrovert discussion first mentioned in the Characterization section. Your demeanor is a communication device. Meyers-Briggs personality testing essentially divides people into introverts or extroverts. Extroverts will usually be happy to communicate with you—often to the point of oversharing. If you're partnered with an introvert, on the other hand, you may have to spend hours prying out of them even the most minor insight into their thoughts and feelings. Introverts and extroverts can work really well together, but they'd better reach some basic understandings on how to communicate first.

How do you solve day-to-day problems?

Do you buckle down and get 'er done? Or do you follow the Scarlett O'Hara school of business and postpone everything, tossing your pretty head and saying, "Tomorrow's another day"? Do you attack problems head-on or think them through carefully? Do you take immediate action, or only when you have a comprehensive plan with every contingency covered? There's no right or wrong—but knowing your problem-solving style can help you communicate better with your partner.

Now define Partnership again. Any changes since you started this section?

What Are We Looking for in this Section?

Your communication style is self-expression, which shows up in everything from the way you dress to the words you use to the way you talk to how you walk in the door at the office. It includes problem solving, stress response and your ability to express and manage your emotions. Understanding each other creates effective communication, which eliminates those deadly ass-umptions, and goes a long way in preventing misunderstandings.

YOUR SELF-EXPRESSION

- Your threshold
- Your temperament
- Your ability to manage your emotions
- Your self-confidence
- Your style
- Your approach to problems

The most basic and powerful way to connect to another person is to listen. Just listen. Perhaps the most important thing we ever give each other is our attention . . . A loving silence often has far more power to heal and to connect than the most well-intentioned words.

—Rachel Naomi Remen

I hope you were honest in this section. You may not like your answers necessarily, but believe me, this area creates the biggest day-to-day challenges. It's like the little habits in a marriage that seem so cute at the beginning ("I just love her enthusiasm!") but end up driving you straight up the wall and through the ceiling ("She's so damn cheery every morning, I'd like to put cyanide in her orange juice").

Exercise

After both partners have answered all the questions in this section and listened to your partner's answers, list the areas of compatibility, conflict and compromise in your partnership and how you will address them. Use the Workbook or as many downloaded Exercise Worksheets as necessary.

Example 11.1

Take a look at this example of healthy communication between Pam and Daniel, partners who are well matched in most ways and have a great partnership. Here's how they work together to solve issues.

COMPATIBILITIES	COMPROMISES	ACTIONS
Both Pam and Daniel are happy people. Pam is the quieter one but can be quite outgoing when she needs to be. Daniel is a loud, boisterous person in just about every situation. He's like Santa Claus, big and jolly. Not much bothers him. Pam is quietly efficient. Daniel is less efficient but a tremendous asset when it comes to client relations.	These two have job descriptions that match their abilities and temperament. They're opposites in many ways, but find each other interesting and balanced rather than finding fault with each other. Both are self-aware and accountable, and comfortable with who they are.	They have created an office culture around being happy. It crosses over into keeping their customers happy too. Pam works internally; Daniel works externally.
CONFLICTS	**COMPROMISES**	**ACTIONS**
Pam gets very quiet when she's stressed. And she dislikes the telephone. It's jarring to her and disrupts her work. *Pam also doesn't like a lot of noise. It disturbs her. She's a writer and needs it quiet.*	The office has been divided into a Pam zone and a Daniel zone. Also, employees are informed of and respect Pam's need for quiet.	The Pam zone is a quiet zone, where nobody is allowed to disturb her. She has created a door-hanger that lets people know whether or not she is available. Additionally, people are urged to communicate with her via email. Daniel welcomes all sorts of visits and calls. He and Pam schedule meetings with each other rather than barging in, which is typical of many partners.

Figure 11.1 *Compatibilities, Conflicts, Compromises and Actions.*

12

#4: COMPENSATION
SOMETHING GIVEN OR RECEIVED

The first step to getting the things you want out of life is this: decide what you want.
—Ben Stein

This section defines what you want from your business, what you bring to it and how it will serve you in terms of financial goals, rewards, lifestyle, status, power, freedom, companionship and eventual exit. Compensation is not just financial, and value is not just measured in dollars. Far from it. Be explicit about what all this means to you and how it will serve you. Put your heart, not just your head, into these answers. And this is not the time to be "nice." Instead, be honest. Finally, bring in the lawyers/financial planner for this section. You will need their expert advice.

QUESTION 1:

Why do you want this business?

Simon Sinek, who wrote *Start With Why*, says this: *People don't buy what you do, they buy why you do it.* His message is one of inspiration. Do what you love; from love comes passion, innovation, endurance, success, longevity and profitability. You do nobody any favors by getting involved in a partnership around a business you don't like or for a reason that isn't about loving what you do.

QUESTION 2:

What exactly do you want from this business? (power, belonging, money, stature, a platform, a big office, lots of toys, etc.)

If you went to buy a home, would you not have a list of demands? Do you not have certain expectations of the person you marry? Do you go back to a restaurant that disappointed you?

To get what you want, say what you want. It's yours to create. And believe me, there are no right or wrong answers. Saying you want power or money or status is just as valid as saying you want to help millions of people change their lives or save the planet. (None of these desires is mutually exclusive, by the way.) Be honest, dammit!

QUESTION 3:

Which best describes you: Mission driven, Vision driven, or Profit driven?

These are three ways of looking at your business personality.

The Mission-driven person wants to achieve the company's stated mission. ("ABC Corp will make the best rivets in all of North Dakota.")

Visionary people see the bigger picture and want to do something more. They want to be better people in a better world for a better cause. ("Our rivets don't just hold the airplanes together; they hold families and lives together. They make it possible for the world to be connected by aviation, and for the workers of North Dakota to be vanguards for global safety.")

Profit-driven people look at one thing only, and that is the bottom line. ("What's the net cost on these rivets and can we make them cheaper in China?") Again, there is no right or wrong here; we need all kinds of people in the world of business. You just need to know what motivates you and to ensure that your partner's motives are in sync with yours.

QUESTION 4:

What exactly does ownership mean to you? (equal split, strategic partner, investor, etc.)

Remember that "equal" is the worst setup and hardly ever works. There can only be one boss, and you're kidding yourself if you think otherwise. Ownership has to be very clearly defined and agreed to by all partners.

Once you have put this into your own words, let the experts give you their stamp of approval. There are tax and other financial and legal ramifications that accompany partnership. Get yourself up to speed so there are no assumptions or costly mistakes.

What exactly does money mean to you? (freedom, power, stature, ability to give, etc.)

As personal development gurus will tell you, none of us wants "money" (unless we're coin collectors)—we want what we think money will give us. Security. Freedom. Power. Position. Possessions. Contribution. The way we expect our business to bring in money will be shaped by what we want that money to do. Someone who seeks status will probably want a really nice office space and a ritzy car. Someone who wants security will be happy to work in a closet and drive a 1999 Ford Taurus to keep expenses down and the company bank account above a certain level. There's no right or wrong in terms of what money means, but it's important to figure out what it means to you. The way a business chooses to make, save and spend its income can create a boatload of disagreements if the partners are looking to get different things from the money the business brings in. Better to learn now what money means to each of you than spend hours or years arguing about it and ultimately giving it all to the lawyers.

What is your money style? (Spend? Save? Invest?)

While you may say, "A little of each," everyone has a primary focus when it comes to money, and trying to change your money style isn't going to last long. A spender is a spender and a saver is a saver. Don't think otherwise.

Know the primary styles of you and your partner so you can deal with it successfully in your business.

Do you see your business as a savings vehicle or a cash machine?

You can see why two people who differ on this would have real, fundamental issues. In my experience, this can be a deal breaker. Should you choose to go ahead with this partner, you're going to need some agreement here.

Ideally your business can be both a way to save for the future and a machine that produces income in the present. But you must build controls into the business to make sure you don't overspend in the happy times, or over-save when you need to spend money today so the business can grow tomorrow.

Are you investing any money in this business/partnership? If so, what?

Are you investing any intellectual or other property in this business/partnership? If so, what?

How will you value that (those) investment(s)?

How will you recoup that (those) investment(s)?

Questions 8 through 11 are critical. Rest assured if you don't clear this up, it will come up—all the time. Be concise about who is investing what and at what value. Everything has a value. The trick is to agree on what that is and how and when it will be repaid. Once you get to the point where you write your Partnership Plan, this will be clearly defined. Again, bring in the lawyer/financial planner for advice. (See Appendix A, Example A, Figure A.1)

What financial compensation do you want from this business? Please be specific about amounts, bonuses, draws, etc.

Put on your employee hat for a minute here. If you were to be the most senior employee at your company, what would you want? Think about your number and then address the issues around it. (See Appendix A, Example A, Figure A.2)

Have you ever filed bankruptcy? If so, why? How was it resolved? Will you document this to an uninvolved third-party professional for verification?

How is your credit? What is your credit score? Will you document this number to an uninvolved third-party professional for verification?

Are you willing to have an uninvolved third-party professional review and confirm your financial statement and /or credit application on all potential partnership bank loans?

Are you willing to purchase life insurance on your potential partner and not cash it in without the other person's knowledge and permission?

Is there anything in your past or present life that could potentially affect this partnership? (illness, legal issues, addiction, financial trouble, incarceration, etc.)

Questions 13 through 17 are all fair game if you're to become partners. It is neither fair nor ethical to saddle someone with your baggage. Be honest and put it out there. If potential partners refuse to answer *any* of these questions, say goodbye and hit the road. Fast. And do not look back.

QUESTION 18:

Define "Success."

QUESTION 19:

Define "Failure."

Again, it's key to know your own definition of these terms as well as your partner's. If your idea of success is a million dollars a quarter and being named *Business of the Year* in your community, you're probably going to work hard but not feel particularly good about any of the small wins along the way. The same might happen if your partner's idea of failure is not getting a "yes" every time the business goes after a new account. The way we define success and failure shapes the way we do business. Get clear on the definitions so you can be clear about your business goals and outcomes. More about that later.

QUESTION 20:

How long can you maintain your interest and participation in this business while it struggles to become profitable?

You will only get paid when the business makes money, and no business makes money at the start. The biggest challenge, however, isn't necessarily the financial wherewithal you both possess to keep things going, but the *emotional* wherewithal you must draw on to keep working even when there's no money coming in and few results to show for your efforts. How much emotional stamina do you possess? How many months can you watch your cash reserves dwindling and your hard work not producing enough results to get your business into the black? How amenable will your spouse be to this?

Choose a reasonable timeframe based on your financial situation and your ability to deal with the stress of having little or no income. (One good thing about partnership: with the right person as your partner, the early, unprofitable, "we're in this together" days of a business are a lot easier to bear, both financially *and* emotionally.)

QUESTION 21:

How do you feel about involving family members in the business?

QUESTION 22:

Do you intend to involve any family members in this business? If so, who, in what positions, and at what compensation package?

Families and small businesses go together like tea and toast. Just be sure you know what your partner wants, and aren't surprised when one day Cousin Andy is running the sales department (which is fine, as long as Andy can do the work—and you build into your partnership a process for dealing dispassionately with underperforming or nonperforming family members).

QUESTION 23:

What's your 10-year life plan?

It's imperative that all potential partners know what the other is thinking. If one wants to retire to a pineapple farm in Hawaii in 10 years and the other wants the company to go public, that's cool. It doesn't mean you can't work together. Not at all. It just means you must put your cards on the table so you can craft an exit strategy that will work for all concerned.

QUESTION 24:

How do you envision this partnership ending? (leave and sell to partner, split and close, selling, merger, etc.)

Plan the end now, with an attorney and financial planner. You can always change it if Coca-Cola comes along and suddenly wants to buy you out. Make sure you decide whether you need to include a non-compete clause if one partner sells his or her share of the business to the other partner(s).

QUESTION 25:

Are you willing to create an exit strategy?

This is the only other question in the P²P Process where "no" is the wrong answer. If a potential partner is not willing to do this, say goodbye.

QUESTION 26:

Now define Partnership again. Has it changed since you started this section?

What are We Looking for in this Section?

This section gets down to the business of business, and how you as a businessperson will act in the proposed partnership. These questions also are designed to get you thinking beyond the fun, "let's put on a show" aspect of starting a business and recognizing the tough times and the long days of lots of work and little money. I also want you to start thinking right now, before you begin this business, about how it's going to end. Answering these serious questions now will help you get things started, (and eventually ended), on the right foot.

YOUR WANTS AND REQUIREMENTS

- Your demands
- Your history
- Your future orientation
- Your business acumen
- Your financial comprehension
- Your financial identity
- Your fiscal temperament

Everything that can be counted does not necessarily count; everything that counts cannot necessarily be counted.

—Albert Einstein

Exercise

After both partners have answered all the questions in this section and listened to your partner's answers, list the areas of compatibility, conflict and compromise in your partnership and how you will address them. Use your Workbook or as many downloaded Exercise Worksheets as necessary.

> **Example 12.1**
>
> This set of questions separates the men from the boys. I will use one of my close friends as an example here. He's far from a boy—he's nearly 50 and should know better.
>
> Paul is a seasoned graphic designer, and although he was busy in his own right, he decided to partner up with someone in his city who could drive some serious business his way. Rob was a mover and shaker in the magazine world, highly regarded, well known in chic circles and very successful. But with changing times comes changing technology, and Paul had the interactive skills Rob needed. So they hitched their wagons and off they went, as 50/50 partners (yikes). Rob joined Paul's already-existing design company (fatal mistake), and they got busy fast. Before they knew it, they had amassed quite a bundle of cash and some nice clients. Over time, they had also decided they could not stand each other.
>
> They went to break up the company, and of course Paul wanted it all back, minus a payout, since it was his in the first place. Except it doesn't work that way. To make matters worse, Paul was also an industrial designer who had created a product before he met Rob but had left it under the corporate umbrella, thinking Rob might be able to help him launch and distribute it. Guess who now owned half the product?
>
> These two had done absolutely no up-front work and their problems were myriad. Besides despising each other, they had zero alignment

in their money philosophy, no mutual vision, no Partnership Plan, formal or informal, and no exit strategy.

The mess this created was epic and could have cost a fortune to litigate. Paul literally had to fight for a product that had nothing to do with Rob but which Rob now owned part of because of no partnership planning. In the end, they dissolved the company, split the revenues and went their separate ways. It cost Paul more to win back his product than the product was ultimately worth. He's back working as a one-man show, bitter and disappointed. One day he will become accountable and realize he had a part in all this. For now, he's knee-deep in blame.

13

#5: CONTRIBUTION
GIVING SOMETHING BACK

Only those who have learned the power of sincere and selfless contribution experience life's deepest joy: true fulfillment.
—Tony Robbins

Are you willing to give back?

If you can be generous to someone, or give back to someone, or pay something forward, you have accomplished the very reason for existence. How important is it to you to create a culture involving contribution, both within your business and between your business and the community?

Often this is the last thing people are thinking about when they start a business: "We can't afford to contribute" or "We'll wait 'til later. We don't have the money now."

It all depends on how you interpret the word "contribution." I firmly believe that great partnerships are all about contribution or they would not be great. It starts with contributing to yourselves, then each other, and then progresses to the partners contributing to the business, to your employees, your customers, your suppliers, and your community. It's not about an amount; it's about the act. Contribution is a mindset rooted in gratitude, and if you have that, you have everything.

QUESTION 1:

What does "giving back" mean to you?

Is it important to you? Why or why not? What does it say about you and your business when you give to others? When you don't?

QUESTION 2:

Do you believe in giving back? Why or why not?

Those who don't believe in giving back are usually either (1) scared they don't have enough to give, or (2) closed off emotionally, perhaps due to some hurtful experiences in the past. Take a careful look at the answer to this question, because a partner who has great reasons for giving back will probably be generous with you. Conversely, someone who perhaps has some reservations about giving back will be less than open or generous in the partnership—and that can make things difficult for you both.

QUESTION 3:

Is it important that your partner(s) be philanthropic? Why or why not?

A shared focus on philanthropy and contribution can strengthen a partnership. However, as in every relationship, it's possible for one party to have an interest that's not shared by the other, and for both to be okay with that. You may feel perfectly fine with a partner who focuses on running the business while you go build homes with Habitat for Humanity. The main thing is to understand and feel good about your partner's perspective on philanthropy, whatever it is, and vice versa.

QUESTION 4:

Is it important that your company be philanthropic? Why or why not?

Will philanthropy be part of your business plan? I think including contribution and philanthropy as elements in your business plan from the very beginning is vital to the health as well as the heart of your enterprise. If that's not true for you, at least make sure both partners are in alignment on this decision.

QUESTION 5:

Would you support college or other intern programs? Why or why not?

QUESTION 6:

Would you sponsor a potential employee for a green card? Why or why not?

Would you be willing to donate some of your business income to a worthy cause? Why or why not?

What causes, entities, or efforts would you be willing for the business to support, with donations of either time or money?

All of these questions will help you both get clear about the kinds of contribution you consider appropriate and valuable. Be specific, not conceptual. If your thing is Best Buddies or Doctors Without Borders, it means you have an emotional attachment, and those are important to nurture. If your partner thinks your charity of choice is a scam, you need to know about it now.

Write a one-sentence statement about contribution.

Come out of you heart on this one. If you can't think of anything, make something up. Mine is "Giving Is Its Own Reward." This could end up being part of your company's vision statement, which you'll be creating later in Section 6: Construction.

Now define Partnership again. Has it changed since you started this section?

What are We Looking for in this Section?

The questions in this section are about much more than philanthropy; they show how generous you and your partner are or plan to be, and how willing you are to involve yourself and your business with the greater community.

YOUR PHILANTHROPIC THRESHOLD

- Your generosity of spirit
- Your level of gratitude
- Your community involvement quotient

I am certain that after the dust of centuries has passed over our cities, we, too, will be remembered not for victories or defeats in battles or on politics, but for our contribution to the human spirit.

—John F. Kennedy

Remember, nobody does business in a vacuum; you have to establish relationships (dare I say, partnerships?) with your customers, suppliers and community. And the better the relationships you build, the more successful your business will become. Giving to others and bringing an attitude of generosity and philanthropy to your partnership will increase not just your success but also your satisfaction. Generosity opens the heart. Philanthropy puts you into relationship with other generous people in the greater community. Sounds like a pretty smart business strategy to me.

Exercise

After both partners have answered all the questions in this section and listened to your partner's answers, list the areas of compatibility, conflict and compromise in your partnership and how you will address them. Use your Workbook or as many downloaded Exercise Worksheets as necessary.

Example 13.1

Interestingly, I have worked with only one partnership team where there was a great divide regarding contribution. This particular team was a good match in most areas except for financial philosophies, so this a great example of how the categories connect and impact each other. It's also a great example of how opposing sides can reach a workable compromise.

Figure 13.1 contains their disconnects regarding financial philosophy and Figure 13.2 shows how those philosophies impact the willingness to contribute, what their resolution was and what action steps they took.

	IS IT IMPORTANT THAT YOUR PARTNER BE PHILANTHROPIC?	IS IT IMPORTANT THE BUSINESS BE PHILANTHROPIC?	WOULD YOU SUPPORT A COLLEGE INTERN PROGRAM?	WOULD YOU DONATE TO A WORTHY CAUSE?	WHAT CAUSE? WITH TIME OR MONEY?
DREW	*No.*	*Not until we reach our revenue goals and even then I'm not sure.*	Sure. Don't interns work for free?	*Not at this time. Have to reach revenue goals first.*	*Our company is my cause.*
PAUL	*Absolutely.*	*Yes absolutely.*	Yes, was a college intern. I got paid.	*Yes.*	*I like OXFAM because I volunteered in college for a summer. They don't just hand out $$ money; they provide knowledge and solutions.*

Figure 13.1 *The challenges of philanthropy. Areas of conflict are in italics.*

CONFLICTS	COMPROMISES	ACTIONS
Drew and Paul are dramatically different when it comes to money and philanthropy. The more absolute of the two is Paul, who is not willing to suspend philanthropy. It's in his blood and his history tells the story (intern/volunteer). Drew has been burned in a prior business but is at heart an entrepreneur and willing to compromise once some of his financial goals for the company have been met. Both are experienced businessmen, and this business together is based on an idea that Drew had. They have a good shot at a successful partnership. Interestingly, this is the only rough area. But what this did is expose tension in the financial area that was not properly expressed during that section's questions. This happens often and is a good example of how the process works interchangeably.	Since Drew is willing to be philanthropic if conditions warrant, they have agreed to work with their CFO to determine Drew's threshold of "cash comfort." Additionally, since there are tax and other benefits that make philanthropy attractive, the CFO will recommend a phased program that will give Paul the satisfaction he needs in this area.	Their first proposed action, once cleared by the CFO, will be to post an OXFAM matching funds link on their website, letting their customers and friends know that they will match donated dollars. Paul believes this will enhance business, a side benefit that will please Drew. They are also considering sponsoring a student Oxfam volunteer to go one of the African nations to serve for 6 months and perhaps teach the logistics business on the company's behalf.

Figure 13.2 *Conflicts, compromises and actions.*

STOP.
GREAT WORK!

DO YOU STILL WANT TO CREATE THIS PARTNERSHIP?

If not, now is the time to say thank you and take a pass.
You have learned much about yourself that will serve you
no matter what you do.

If you've made it this far and are still committed to being
partners, you have just created a solid Human Foundation.

Congratulations.

Now it's time to build on it and build your business.

CREATE YOUR BUSINESS:

THE FINAL P^{2}P CATEGORIES

14

#6: CONSTRUCTION
BUILDING THE BUSINESS YOU WANT

A business has to be involving, it has to be fun,
and it has to exercise your creative instincts.
—Richard Branson

Most would-be partners never think about building the Human Foundation before they take the steps covered in the next pages. In fact, most would-be partners don't do any of these steps. They do what I did: simply get a great idea, find someone who also thinks it's a great idea, get a business license and a company name, and get to it. Face it: that's pretty much like meeting someone in a bar in Vegas and waking up married. Not usually a recipe for a successful long-term relationship but a great recipe for Partnersh*t!

However, if you've made it this far, you're ahead of the curve. You and your partner understand each other more than many married couples do. You've laid the groundwork for a quality personal and professional relationship. The next step is to apply some of the same kind of rigorous preparation to creating the business of your business. The Human Foundation is in place; you're on the same page. Now you can properly build a business that makes you both proud.

In this section, you're going to need tangible answers—real, dollar-making thoughts and ideas. You and your partner will look for alignment in your visions regarding what this business should look like, what it will produce and how it will make money. This section is the beginning of your business plan.

+ + + + + + +

What business are you in?

This is a critical question, so define, define define, and dig, dig, dig. Drill down to the essence of *why exactly* you are creating this business, and come up with a clear statement of *what exactly* you want your business to be about. For example, you might be in the restaurant business, but the business you are really in is helping people get healthy through proper nourishment from whole, healthy foods. Or maybe the business you are really in is creating a social atmosphere for people to get together and enjoy themselves. It's the same business—a restaurant—but with completely different spotlights that will produce very different experiences for both the owners and the customers. Your success will come from having a clear understanding of what your purpose is in starting this business.

QUESTION 2:

Why are you in this business?

The reason you want to go into this business is one of the most important things to discover, because it will give you the emotional drive to keep going when things get tough. Perhaps your father died from obesity, so healthy eating is an emotional trigger for you. Maybe you grew up on a farm and loved being in the fields with all the fresh fruits and vegetables. Or your uncle always owned restaurants and became famous because of it, and you idolized him. Get to the *human* heart of this matter.

QUESTION 3:

Does this business or the idea of this business fulfill your expectations/desires? Why or why not?

If not, you have some work to do . . . or you might want to consider a different business.

QUESTION 4:

Is there anything lacking in this business that might take your interest away from it? If so, what?

If so, now's the time to build it in (or abandon the idea altogether). Your business will be one of the most time- and energy-consuming entities in your life, especially at the beginning, so you'd better be willing to go all in.

The next two questions are vital for creating clarity around your business. Businesses need a mission and a vision statement. Along with values, this is the triumvirate of business building that goes hand in hand with your human foundation to hold up the business.

The best explanation I have ever seen about the difference between vision and mission is this: Add "–ary" to the end of each word.

VisionARY: A visionary is someone who sees what is possible.

MissionARY: A missionary is someone who carries out the work.

You need both vision and mission for a successful business—a vision statement of where you want to go and then a mission statement to describe how you will get there.

QUESTION 5:

Describe your *vision* for the business in one sentence.

A vision statement is a clear, motivating message about what you want the future of your organization to look like. It should be a vivid, inspirational and energizing mental picture. And it must be transformational. This is your vision for the business.

Example 14.1

Chevron: *At the heart of The Chevron Way is our vision … to be the global energy company most admired for its people, partnership and performance.*

IKEA:	*The IKEA vision is to create a better everyday life for the many people.*
Boeing:	*People working together as one global enterprise for aerospace leadership.*
Office Depot:	*Delivering Winning Solutions that Inspire Worklife*™

QUESTION 6:

What is the *mission* of your business?

Your mission statement makes your vision practical. It shows how your business will accomplish the vision. Look at the difference between the vision statements above and the following counterpart mission statements.

Example 14.2

Chevron:	Our Company's foundation is built on our Values, which distinguish us and guide our actions. We conduct our business in a socially responsible and ethical manner. We respect the law, support universal human rights, protect the environment, and benefit the communities where we work.
IKEA:	IKEA's mission is to offer a wide range of home furnishing items of good design and function, excellent quality and durability, at prices so low that the majority of people can afford to buy them.
Boeing:	Become the dominant player in commercial aircraft and bring the world into the jet age.

Office Depot approaches this differently. Theirs is more a core values statement, and they are focused on excellence.

Respect For The Individual
- *We value diversity across the Company.*
- *We praise publicly and provide constructive feedback privately. We listen; we understand and we are responsive to each other.*
- *We treat every employee, customer and supplier with honesty, dignity and respect.*
- *We provide a safe environment to work and shop.*
- *We are committed to the principles of good corporate citizenship, positive social impact and environmental sustainability.*

Fanatical Customer Service
- *We impress our customers (internal and external) so much that they want to buy again.*
- *We give higher priority to people than to tasks.*
- *We do it right the first time but "wow" our customers on recovery when we miss.*

Excellence in Execution
- *We are committed to grow*

Shareholder Value
- *We consistently involve employees at all levels toward the relentless improvement of our business.*
- *We hold ourselves and our teammates accountable for results.*
- *We strive for perfect execution every day.*
- *We reward innovation and intelligent risk taking.*
- *We celebrate the wins.*

The process of developing vision and mission statements is something you and your partner must do together. Once you have your vision and mission statements, you're ready to get very practical in terms of how your vision and mission will play out in the near future.

Write your Onliness Statement

What's that? Only the coolest, most focused piece of writing that you will ever create for your brand / product. Its creator, esteemed brand consultant Marty Neumeier, says that if you cannot briefly state what makes your brand or product different from the competition, then you need to go back to the drawing board.

His short formula is this:

Our brand (product) is the only _____ that/who _____ .

Perhaps the best example of a short-form Onliness Statement would be this one, written about Neumeier's book, *Zag*, by Bloomberg Business Week's Jesse Scanlon:

"(Neumeier) is the only **design and brand expert** who **writes big-idea books filled with practical how-to advice designed to be read on a brief plane ride.**"

While this is brilliant, I believe it's important to narrow the focus. So I prefer that my clients go all the way, using Neumeier's longer version. This elaboration will also pinpoint your purpose and market.

Here is an example of the same Onliness Statement, but in the longer format:

What:	The only design and brand expert
How:	who writes big-idea books
Who:	for people who insist on brand excellence
Where:	anywhere brands, products or businesses exist
Why:	who want practical how-to advice
When:	they can read on a brief plane ride.

This statement will get you focused like nothing else. Take Neumeier's advice on this one. If you cannot identify what makes you unique, then you are not, and your chances of product failure or at best, mediocrity, are high.

What are your three most important goals for the next year?

What are those goals dependent upon? What has to happen to achieve those goals?

With these two questions, you and your partner should be able to come up with the beginnings of an action plan for the year. Goals must be specific, realistic, achievable and actionable. If this is a new business or you are new to business, you might not want to declare that you will do $10 million and expand into 10 countries. Do not set goals that you cannot achieve. Goals have to be based on practical, financial and industry-specific information and research.

Look ahead to the future and write a scenario incorporating your most fervent wishes for this business.

Include desires, hopes, dreams, dollars, locations, dream clients, expansion ideas, fancy company cars, trips or anything else you want to create. Where this gets really interesting is when you compare your fervent wishes with those of your partner. You may find yourself inspired or intimidated or even confused by your partner's dreams. But how important do you think it is to share similar dreams and wishes for your business?

Example 14.3

One of my clients wants to be the Richard Branson of the photography business. To do this, his dream is to open a huge studio that would create a lease-out revenue stream, get booked by Chanel, have Anna Wintour beg him to shoot for *Vogue*, and the rest will be history. He wants and has worked hard for the lights-camera-action that could pull him into the celebrity world and make him the go-to guy in his field. If only . . .

His partner was apoplectic when she heard this. She has a young family and her dream is to build a steady, manageable business with no overhead. She's looking to create a secure future, one in which she can be insanely creative in her work, insanely secure in her finances and insanely private in her personal life.

What is interesting here is that because of the P²P Process, they realized how far apart their dreams were. These two are committed to their partnership and were open to solving this issue. Ironically, because they were able to unearth these dreams and talk about them, in the end they are both now getting what they want. He is fast becoming the go-to guy without having to invest in the heavy overhead. And she is more creative, secure and happily private than ever before.

QUESTION 11:

How soon will this happen?

It's important to check in to see whether your idea of "soon" is the same as your partner's—your "soon" may be five years while your partner's is 20. More important, this question can demonstrate how idealistic or realistic each partner is when it comes to how much and how quickly you can grow this business. There's nothing wrong if one partner is more conservative while the other is aggressive—in fact, there are benefits to having both perspectives in a partnership. But knowing each partner's attitudes will help you avoid arguments about risk taking, investing, long-term versus short-term planning, and so on.

QUESTION 12:

Look ahead to the future and write a scenario incorporating the worst that could happen in this business.

Include everything that would make you sad, angry, disappointed, scared or feel like a failure. Most businesses don't do this kind of planning, and it's a mistake to leave it out. Looking the tiger of the worst-case scenario in the eye and deciding that you can deal with it will make you, your partner, and your business stronger.

What would you do or how far would you go to avoid having that scenario ever happen?

Having envisioned the worst, now you can plan how you can avoid it. Here's the truth, though: worst-case scenarios usually call for drastic action. And you have to be very clear on exactly how far you would be willing to go to save your business. Be specific but realistic. Don't say things like, "If the business got into financial trouble I'd sell everything I own to keep it going" if you have a family that's depending on you and they're your highest priority. When it came right down to it, could you really see your spouse and your kids sitting on the curb because you sold your house to finance the business? If the answer is yes, good for you. But you'd better know in advance exactly how far you'd go.

What are We Looking for in this Section?

This is the "big picture" of your business—and it's a lot more important than the number of widgets you plan to sell or where you're going to rent your first office.

YOUR PURPOSE

- Your business description
- Your fears
- Your sense of reality
- Your brand goals
- Your expectations

The vision, mission, purpose, dreams and fears you have for your

When you are inspired by some great purpose, some extraordinary project, all your thoughts break their bonds; Your mind transcends limitations, your consciousness expands in every direction, and you find yourself in a new, great and wonderful world. Dormant forces, faculties and talents become alive, and you discover yourself to be a greater person by far than you ever dreamed yourself to be.

—Patanjali

business will drive you every single day. They will shape the way you find and serve your customers. By completing these questions, you have put a solid "framework" on top of the Human Foundation you've already built. With work and focus, it's a framework that will stand the test of time.

Exercise

After you have answered all the questions in this section and listened to your partner's answers, list the areas of compatibility, conflict and compromise in your partnership and how will you address them. Use your Workbook or as many of the downloaded Exercise Worksheets as necessary.

15

THE THE P²P PLAN
THE HOME STRETCH

He and I were about as compatible as a rat and a boa constrictor.
—Stevie Nicks, on Fleetwood Mac band member
and ex-boyfriend Lindsey Buckingham

By now you should be clear where your areas of friction and of compatibility lie, and you know that friction, properly managed, isn't a deal breaker. It might be a PITA, but you can handle it. So it's not so scary anymore, is it? Sure, Stevie Nicks and Lindsay Buckingham had some explosive times and monster breakups, but you gotta think they learned something over the years, because Fleetwood Mac still performs together today, at their convenience. I saw them in concert not so long ago and together they are otherworldly. Partnerships are like that. They are bigger than the people in them. That's why they are so important and need such care. Partners feed off each other, creating an energy that is beyond explanation. Yes, often it's explosive, but explosions don't have to be fatal. Properly managed, they can clear out the debris and make room for the new and improved.

To get to this point in the P²P Process, you've talked, you've argued, you've laughed, you've been frustrated, you've felt stupid, you've thought you're wasting time, you've been tired of this whole thing, maybe you've cried—but you have listened. To yourselves and each other. And you're ready to go for it.

You already know that -sh*t only goes one way, and that is down. It's time to build your -ship that will be strong, sturdy and will stay afloat.

So now what?

Well, to answer, I go back to my roots. Again, process. Take process that extra step further: when you feel the information in your body, as you undoubtedly have during this process (sick to your stomach, angry, joyful, etc.) the impact is not just more powerful, but enduring. This is known as integration. You remember how something feels, as in the where-were-you-when-the-planes-hit-the-towers feeling. You will never forget.

Remember Kevin and Keith? Aside from full-out participating in this process, they

1. Integrated the information by physically feeling both the pain and joy they were causing themselves and each other, and

2. Created their Partnership Plan and graphically hung some of its key sections on their wall, like art, for all, including them, to see.

Wall or not, we're going to do the same thing.

FIRST, INTEGRATE WHAT YOU HAVE LEARNED

Answer these questions honestly and completely. You will be held accountable to these promises, so declare yourselves with full, honorable intent. Make your answers compelling. Say what you mean and mean what you say. Make sure this comes from your heart and not your head. *Your partner and everyone around you will be able to tell the difference.*

As always, write the answers down in your Workbook or on the worksheet. You'll be sharing them with your partner at the end of this chapter.

1. My reason(s) for doing this process was/were…

Write as much or as little as you want. Just make sure you write from your heart.

_____

_____

_____

2. The 10 keywords that I heard when I LISTENED to my partner speak during this process are:

1. _____

2. _____

3. _____

4. _____

5. _____

6. _____

7. _____

8. _____

9. _____

10._____

3. The five most important distinctions that I made (about anything) during the P^{2}P Process, in order of importance, are:

1. _____

2. _____

3. _____

4. _____

5. _____

4. To honor those distinctions, I will commit to the following:

1. _____

2. _____

3. _____

4. _____

5. _____

5. The top three things I will commit to so I can passionately empower this partnership are:

1. _____

2. _____

3. _____

6. When we hit a bump, I will...

_____

_____

_____

6. I have learned from and am acknowledging, honoring, respecting and empowering my partner, and myself right here, right now, because...

_____

_____

_____

_____

Now take a break.

Take a walk or go out for a glass of wine with your partner(s) and share the answers you just wrote down. Talk to each other about everything you've learned. Give each other written copies of this integration document. It's a general synopsis that will make sure both of you stay on track and will be a reminder of the value you've gotten from the P²P Process. You can refer to it when things get bumpy, as they inevitably will. Sh*t happens, even in the best partnership, so it's good to have reminders like this to keep things clean.

Then, take a few days to be on your own to think. Maybe even a week or two. This is a hugely important step. All this information needs to percolate. I've discovered that clarity comes to my clients when they step away and give the process the air it needs to breathe. The cream will rise to the top, as it always does. Trust it.

YOUR PARTNERSHIP PLAN

You are now ready to write your Partnership Plan. It will be a constant reminder to us about how important this partnership is to you, your partner, your success, your future, your families and everyone else who is part of your business.

The answered questions give you everything you need to write your Partnership Plan. With your partner, review Section A and then create your own draft of everything you want and agree on. You will find Partnership Plan examples in Appendix A. When you are satisfied with the document, take it to an attorney for perspective, legality and most important, the legalities behind a solid exit strategy. However, make this YOUR document, not your attorney's. Legalese will not have an impact on your emotions; talk that comes straight from your heart will. The more human it is, the deeper you will feel it and the stronger it will be. The lawyers can add their input after you are done so it passes the legal smell test.

I also recommend meeting with an accountant or other financial professional for relevant advice after you create your draft. It takes a team. Really, it does. (I wanted to say village but that's just too timeworn and obvious.)

Once all the "suits" have reviewed the document and done any fine-tuning, you and your partner will sign it. In blood, if you have to. This document is a living, breathing thing, here to guide you, ground you, relieve you and save you. Make sure to build in times to review your agreement, at the very least, annually. Don't feel you have to wait for scheduled reviews to consult this document. Go back to it—often. Adjust it as you and the business grow and change. Consider your Partnership Plan a kind of vow, and pay as much attention to these vows as you do your marriage vows (unless they are meaningless to you, in which case, hmmmm).

With your Partnership Plan next to your business vision and mission statement, you and your partner are ready for the next step. You're ready to move on to create your business framework using using Osterwalder's Business Model Canvas Tool, which will help you develop:

1. Your Business Strategy

2. Your Branding Strategy

3. Your Marketing Strategy

16

#7: CREATION
DESIGNING THE BUSINESS YOU WANT

Imagination is the beginning of creation. You imagine what you desire, you will what you imagine and at last you create what you will.
—George Bernard Shaw

While this is a book on partnership, it is incumbent upon me to complete the picture. After having created a Human Foundation and a solid vision and mission for their business, many people don't know what to do next. Others do know but perhaps can benefit from some reminders of what's needed. Either way, I want to finish the job at hand by sharing some of the tools I use with my clients to create the businesses they want.

In this final stage, you will turn the *dream* of your business into something tangible and real.

Let me say at this point that, while I am an expert in creating the Human Foundation and Brand Strategy, I go to other experts to help me with business and some marketing strategies, particularly as it relates to search engine optimization and marketing (SEO/SEM). Online is where everything is headed.

I'm going to give you some of the highlights in each of four areas: (1) Business Model Canvas, (2) Business Strategy, (3) Brand Strategy and (4) Marketing Strategy, and then point you in the direction of the experts who I believe are the best in their respective fields. You can follow up with them, read their books, take their courses and use their tools. I have, and can testify to the quality of their work. I also want you to know that I am not a paid affiliate for any of the books, processes or people that I recommend. I'm just a happy customer who recommends them because they helped me enormously and I hope they help you too.

Remember the diagram on page 85? Here it is again. This is the process I follow.

Figure 16.1 *Osterwalder's Business Model Canvas*

1. CREATE YOUR BUSINESS MODEL CANVAS®

By now you understand I'm not just a builder; I'm also a creator. I think it's important to create your business the way you want it; first, so it makes you happy, and second, for the ultimate benefit of your customers. Creation guarantees that clarity, humanity, heart and soul get put into the recipe, not just a business plan or customer analysis.

I am a huge proponent of a tool called Osterwalder's Business Model Canvas® (BMC®). I use this not just for every company I help create but on every project I do, whether for myself or for my clients. I have found this to be the most useful strategic tool I have ever used.

BMC is a framework that sets the stage for you to systematically and purposefully view and parse your thoughts and ideas, ultimately leading you to the basis for your business and marketing strategies.

The brilliance of BMC lies in its simplicity. The canvas is created around the idea of innovation and is direct, compelling and thought provoking. You can see your business or project for what it really is, right in front of you, all on one simple grid on one page. Perhaps the most important innovation is the strategic visual execution, rather than the outdated long, boring document creation that most people won't read anyway.

The BMC will help you determine the following:

- What is your Value Proposition, i.e., what do you bring to the party and why is it different?
- Who are your Key Customers?
- What sort of relationship do you want to have with those Key Customers?
- What Key Activities do you need to do to execute your Value Proposition for your Key Customers?
- What Key Resources do you need to fulfill those Key Activities so you can execute your Value Proposition for your Key Customers?
- What Channels will you use to reach your Key Customers?
- Who are the Key Partners who can help you?
- Where are your Revenue Streams?
- What are your Costs?

My strong recommendation is that your next step, right now, is to use the BMC to begin creating your business. As with the Human Foundation, you can either do this yourself or contact my office—we have qualified trainers who can help you.

I also urge you to download the Business Model Canvas (http://www. businessmodelgeneration.com/canvas) and buy its accompanying book, *Business Model Generation: A Handbook for Visionaries, Game Changers and Challengers*. It's a great addition to any office library. This group also has a sensational sharing website (www.businessmodelgeneration.com) and a powerful online community (www.businessmodelgeneration.com/hub).

And talk about a partnership. The authors, Alexander Osterwalder and Yves Pigneur, collaborated with 470 (nope, that is not a typo) strategists from 45 countries to create and refine this innovative tool. Their community mindset is the future of partnerships.

Example 16.1

LR Storage Corporation.

This new partnership wanted to set up a new business around a unique storage concept. We spent three sessions taking the concept apart to see just what launching the business would entail. The partners were able to see at a glance just how much work was necessary to get this business going. Additionally, the partners were intimately involved in analyzing and planning each and every category. The Business Model Canvas sparked their creative thinking so they were able to come up with innovations they had not thought about before. It also laid everything out for the next step, which is defining the Business Strategy. See Figure 16.2 on the next page.

THE BUSINESS MODEL CANVAS

Designed for:
LR Storage Corp.

Designed by:
Soffer Collective Branding + Design

KEY PARTNERS

IT Developer
Leasing Partner
Creative Partner
Transport Company Partner
Insurance Companies-Referrals
Investors
Outsourced Services Co's.
Construction Companies
Habitat for Humanity and other charitable organizations
Closet Companies

KEY ACTIVITIES

Set up Partnership
Create Product Workflow
Develop Software/ App
Secure Warehouse Space
Develop Logistics
Create Branding + Messaging
Design
Marketing
Customer Development

KEY RESOURCES

Intellectual Resources:
Proprietary Software
Proprietary Logistics System
Human Resources:
Key People
Physical Resources:
Proprietary Real Estate

VALUE PROPOSITIONS

White Glove Service
Valet Service
Technology-based
Online Requisition System
App
Barcoding of individual items, not just boxes
Store "By the Box"
Secure, clean, temperature controlled
Pick-up/Deliver
We pack or you pack
Option: Code and Catalog and store everything in customer's own closet
Vacation Clean-up Service

CUSTOMER RELATIONSHIPS

Personal assistance and service
"Cool" factor
Hi-tech access/automated services with online access
We are a problem solver for our customers
User community

CHANNELS

Web-based customer interface
Internet marketing
App
Suggestion Box
WOM testimonials
Eblast/eEmarketing
Collateral
On-truck advertising
Branded boxes
Branded building

CUSTOMER SEGMENTS

1. Customers who value service, convenience and organization
   - High-end closet customers
   - Overcrowded closets
   - Newly married
   - Downsizing
   - New baby/growing family
   - Want own closet organized
2. Seasonal Customers
   - The Owner's Closet
   - Seasonal garments
   - College storage
3. Crisis Customers
   - Home renovations
   - Construction
   - Water/flood damaged
   - Relocations
4. Other Storage Companies
   - Relieve overcrowding
   - Act as repository

COST STRUCTURE

HR: Staffing/training
Legal
Insurance
Capital Costs
Real Estate
Equipment

Platform Development/Management
Logistics Development
IT Development
Software Development
Marketing/Advertising/PR
Customer Acquisition and Maintenance

REVENUE STREAMS

1. Intellectual Property:
   - Software Fees/Royalties/ Usage Fees
2. Service Revenue:
   - Annual Subscriptions
   - Code, Catalog, Crate Fees
   - Pickup + Delivery Fees
   - Storage Fees
   - Quick-Turnaround
   - Special Scheduled Delivery

3. Strategic Alliance Revenue
   - Insurance Companies
   - Real Estate Brokers
   - Closet Companies
   - Moving Companies
   - Other Storage Companies
   - Customer Referral Programs

www.businessmodelgeneration.com (used with permission)

Figure 16.2 *Sample Business Model Canvas.*

2. CREATE YOUR BUSINESS STRATEGY

Business strategy is a skill unto itself and requires the same attention, breadth of vision and focus you have put into your Human Foundation. Because this is not my area of expertise, I have worked with many strategists, attended workshops and have read book after book on the subject. I believe in going to the best there is.

Business strategy is essentially this: You must determine where you are now and where you want to be in X years. The strategy, then, is to define how to get there.

You don't have to do this alone. You have a friend in The Kauffman Foundation, a nonprofit organization whose mission is to understand the phenomenon of entrepreneurship, to advance entrepreneurship education and training efforts, to promote entrepreneurship-friendly policies, and to better facilitate the commercialization of new technologies by entrepreneurs and others, to improve economic welfare. This is a gem of a resource for any entrepreneurial business owner. Their website (www.kauffman.org) is a veritable gold mine of small business information, guidance and resources. The free, downloadable PDFs alone will help you get started, master growth, innovate and connect with community.

Kauffman also features several initiatives for entrepreneurs, including:

- FasTrac, (http://fasttrac.org/), a sensational repository of programs that help entrepreneurs create and grow their businesses;
- Kauffman Labs, (http://www.kauffmanlabs.org/, which teaches and trains new and next-generation entrepreneurs in a lab setting;
- iStart, (http://istart.org/), for those of you who want to enter business competitions, browse pages of startup ideas or network with other entrepreneurs;
- iBridge, (http://www.ibridgenetwork.org/), a killer university research database;
- Kauffman Scholars, (http://www.kauffmanscholars.org/) and

the Urban Entrepreneur Partnership (http://www.kauffman. org/entrepreneurship/urban-entrepreneur-partnership.aspx) serve students and business owners in the urban core.

- Kauffman is also seriously invested in sustainable businesses and community building. Take a look at their Energy Innovation Network, (http://www.energyinnovationnetwork.org/).

If you are of a seminar mindset, my gold-star recommendation would be to invest in Tony Robbins' Business Mastery Seminar. The man is not just the most inspiring and heartfelt person I have ever met but ranks as one Accenture's "Top 50 Business Intellectuals in the World" and "Top 200 Business Gurus" by Harvard Business School Press.

Robbins gathers experts from the business world to help him teach, and these are impressive people. Vegas tycoon Steve Wynn spoke at one event, as did Zappos' Tony Hsieh, and my favorite business guru Keith Cunningham is always there to impart his practical and often hilarious wisdom on how to achieve measurable financial results. (http://www. keystothevault.com/). You might also run into marketing geniuses Frank Kern, John Carlton and Jay Abraham, master thought leader Tom Wujek and others. It all depends on the curriculum. The seminar teaches business mapping, strategy, innovation techniques, marketing, sales, finance, legalities, business optimization and customer satisfaction, along with doses of inspiration to be the best businessperson you can be.

It's a place where you and your partner(s) can build or grow the business together, in a room full of business masters who are there to serve and operate from their hearts. This is a fantastic addition to your Human Foundation.

There are other, less costly seminars that you can attend and strategists you can hire who are independent of the seminar world. Do your research and get recommendations before you hit that payment button.

Lastly, you can model an organization you admire. People love to talk, so if there is a business out there that resonates with you, pick up the phone and call them. Let them know how you feel about their business and ask if you can talk to someone about how they strategized it. While nobody will divulge trade secrets, people will talk about what they did to become great, because they are proud of it.

Whatever your choice, don't be afraid to ask. Business isn't easy, and the greatest business people never stop learning. It's the only way to stay sharp.

3. CREATE YOUR BRAND STRATEGY

Branding is where you get to create how your business looks, feels and competes and is always a favorite with my clients. The Branding Process is fun! Obviously I love it, since it has been my life's work, and you'd *better* love what you do.

While our company's process is an amalgamation of several brilliant branding minds and has been built and modified over time, my favorite guru is Alina Wheeler, who wrote what I consider to be *the* book on branding.

Designing Brand Identity: An Essential Guide for the Whole Branding Team, now in its Third Edition, is customer-centric and super user-friendly. I do recommend you hire a good brand strategy/marketing team to guide you through the process (there's that word again). The book is simply there to explain the fundamentals in plain visual and written language, and to inspire creativity. Wheeler is up-to-date on the tools and media evolutions of the day yet stands by her deep respect for the long-held fundamentals.

Wheeler will tell you herself: No one does this alone. Branding is a collective process. You need business brains and design brains in the same room. And don't forget your customer when you go through the branding process—your customer must always be top of mind because ultimately, a brand is not what you say it is. It's what your customer says it is.

To create a coherent brand identity (one that holds together and that all people understand), there are five strategic stages:

A. RESEARCH PHASE

Once again, asking the right questions and listening (in this case, to your key stakeholders) is key to getting the right answers. By now you should be an expert at this! Some of this will

> WHAT I HAVE LEARNED IS THIS:
>
> **THE BRAND THAT IS DEEPEST IN YOUR CUSTOMER'S HEART WILL WIN.**

sound familiar because we covered it in Section #6: Construction. If you have completed the P²P Process, you already have quite a head start. To create a strong brand for your company, you must develop and understand:

- Who you are
- What business you are in
- Your mission and vision
- Your strengths and weaknesses
- Your key stakeholders
- Your product(s)
- Your target market
- Your competition
- Your competitive advantage
- How you will organize your company
- Your office/ corporate culture
- Near-and long-term goals

B. STRATEGIC AND CLARIFICATION PHASE

In this phase, you must exercise your analytical, rational and creative sides.

Take a strategic look around to see what's up out there in the world, where your customers and competition live and where you will be doing business.

1. Understand your Brand

    a. What is your marketing strategy? (You will learn how to build this in the next section.)

    b. What are the general industry, cultural and political trends?

    c. How will you price your product?

    d. How will you distribute?

2. Voice your Brand

    a. Create your Brand Brief

    This document solidifies the understanding of your brand.

    b. Create your Creative Brief

    This is your brand road map. Once approved by the key members of your brand team, the creative brief will keep you focused and on track as you develop creative in the next step.

3. Name your Brand

The name's the thing. Your company's name is an asset, as are employees, clients, products and fixtures. Some companies start a company based on a name; most companies name a company based on "aggravated" agreement—people just give in so they can move on. No. Don't do that. Naming is a process like everything else. Give it its due. A name should stand out, explain something and be unforgettable. It must reflect the goals and positioning you have set for the company and tell a story. If you use a made-up name (Google; Zillow; Kodak; TiVo), that's cool, but understand it will require a symphony of brand power and dollars to communicate its meaning.

C. DESIGN PHASE

This is the phase in which most businesses start. No! No! No! You do NOT need a logo and a website UNTIL you have done ALL of the above work including (all you partners out there) the P²P Process. I cannot stress this enough. How do you expect to decorate the living room when you have yet to build the house?

Once you have done all the prep work, this is where your brand becomes visual. Understand that design, properly executed, is as strategic and scientific as creating a spreadsheet (but way more fun). Give this phase the respect it deserves in the form of a solid brand and creative brief and a killer name/tagline, and it will repay you in spades. If you don't, I hate to tell you the cost of redesign once you realize that fancy new logo and site have nothing to do with what or to whom you are selling. Now is not the time to let your 12-year-old cousin show you his skills, unless he is a prodigy of Pentagram or Landor caliber. Look them up. You'll see strategic branding par excellence.

You'll be looking to do the following in this phase:

1. Create your color palette.
- Color is a science and colors elicit emotions, memories, associations and behaviors from people. Make sure what you choose represents the goals you have in mind.

2. Define tyopgraphy
- I haven't counted, but I will guess there are somewhere between 10 and 20,000 typefaces out there. Type is as important to branding as water is to life.

3. Create the logo/symbol
- This graphic representation of your company's name is your anchor. People think in pictures first, and your logo will root them to your brand—good or bad. Famed graphic

designer Milton Glaser says, "The logo is the gateway to the brand." Alina Wheeler says that the best identities advance the brand and are inexorably tied to ideals, meaning, authenticity, differentiation, durability, value, flexibility, coherence and commitment. And it will take time to achieve all this. So nope, it's not just another pretty design. It is a strategic business tool, and adherence to its promise must be a relentless business practice.

4. Define the voice for video and audio.

- It's a new age. Video and audio are it. Websites are video-driven today, and many products, especially service-oriented products, are downloaded or sold as DVDs. Pay sharp attention to both the message and the messenger.

5. Test.

- Make sure what you have created works across the brand. The logo must be scalable; appropriate for all media including and especially the web; legible at all sizes; adaptable in color and black/white; accommodative of a tagline if appropriate; adaptable to other cultures.

D. DEVELOPMENT PHASE

In this phase, you take care of protecting your brand and all your hard work via trademarking (™), service marking (SM), or copywriting (©). You can do this online via www. uspto.gov and www.copyright.gov, www.Legalzoom.com or call your attorney for assistance. It's also time to create the brand extensions. The possibilities are virtually endless and dependent upon the business you are in, but here are some of the more common branded items:

- Letterhead Set
- Business Card

- Website
- Apps
- Web Favicons
- Brochures or other printed collateral
- Signage
- Product Packaging
- Ads
- Environmental Graphics
- Uniforms
- Other stuff called "Ephemera"

You are preparing to take a bow in front of your audience, who will soon have the opportunity to get to know how you feel, taste, smell, look, sound, contribute and cost. Never lose an opportunity to brand your company. From trucks to tee shirts to tattoos, the more you are in front of the customer, the more they will keep you top of their mind. Put a brand on it!

E. MANAGEMENT PHASE

Like anything else, your brand requires tender loving care. Just as you cannot create a winning partnership and then not pay attention to it, so too must you always keep your eye on the brand ball. It's a living, breathing entity that will grow and change over time. Yes, your business might be selling tires or operating a shoe store, but it still all comes down to brand. What do you stand for? What did you promise? Why did you attract the customers in the first place? How is your retention? What are the complaints?

Your customers will come back time and again if you live up to your promises, make them feel like kings, stay ahead with innovation and deliver a consistent experience.

I always recommend that my clients develop a Brand Book, which highlights the brand standards and guidelines. I have posted a sample on my website (ahumanfoundation.com/downloads). Many small businesses don't want to go to the extra time or cost of producing one but in my experience, it's not just a brand tool but also an employee tool. I come from the school of "if you write something down, it becomes real." I believe a Brand Book rallies and unifies employees. As well as being a handy point of reference for your vendors, which means cutting down on phone calls, email and questions, it's also a tangible reminder of what the company is all about and why they choose to work there.

Finally, this is where you roll out the brand to your customers. Your launch is a strategy in itself that requires massive thought and consideration. It's your debut! You don't want to go out there with lipstick on your teeth. Use the Business Model Canvas to plan it. It's the perfect tool.

In the end, you must always be a customer first. Put on your customer hat and think about your favorite businesses: What do they do that keeps you coming back? Think about those who you have abandoned: What didn't they do? Why did you leave them? This is all valuable information. The smart business owner never forgets why he's there. And he always measures.

F. MEASUREMENT PHASE

Measurement is critical. You must set up categories of measurement as part of both your business and brand plans. The type of business you are in will determine your categories, and of course this criteria must be defined by a CFO, but generally speaking, you should look at:

- Cash flow
- Customer behavior
- Market Share
- Loyalty

- Revenue per customer
- Sales projections
- Response rates
- Web analytics
- Social media analytics
- Employee performance and retention

Obviously there are things that cannot be "measured" in the acceptable sense but nonetheless are critical to a brand's success or failure. Some of these are:

- Perception
- Pride
- Public Relations
- Satisfaction
- Sustainability
- Community standing

How long will all this take? There is no clear-cut answer. Like everything else in this book, it's a process. And the timeliness of it will depend on many factors:

- How allied the partners are *
- How good your communication skills are *
- How big your company is
- How complex your product is to produce
- How much research is required
- How many markets you plan to serve
- How fluid your decision process is*
- How complete your team is*
- Complexity of legal issues, if any

(*Now that you have built your Human Foundation, you should be a master in these areas. You can see how misalignment between the principals and bad communication skills will kill a good product and/or business. You have learned via the P²P Process how to overcome both.)

4. CREATE YOUR MARKETING STRATEGY

This final strategy goes hand-in-hand with your branding strategy. There is always overlap in these areas. Some do the marketing strategy before the brand strategy. I believe strongly in developing all the parts of the brand's story first, which reveals a thorough understanding of the market, before focusing on marketing. Branding is a strategy that drives not just the marketing but also operations, management, sales and the company's culture. That said, often the marketing strategy will reveal itself during brand development. Remember—it's a process.

I can best explain the difference between the two like this:

- *Branding* is creating an identity.

- *Marketing* is managing the promise of that identity by taking the product(s) from concept to the customer, plus satisfying and keeping the customer.

Marketing is the core of your business growth. The secret doesn't lie in the price; it lies in the value you deliver. Market that value and meet the needs of your customers, and always be sure to innovate. Apple is the best example of this that exists anywhere. They create products we didn't know we needed. They market to our emotions and make us feel important and part

> WHAT I HAVE LEARNED IS THIS:
>
> CUSTOMERS WILL PAY GOOD MONEY TO FEEL IMPORTANT, SO MAKE THEM FEEL IMPORTANT.

of a community by owning the product. They continue to innovate with more must-have products. They are the masters of the marketing universe and we can all take a lesson from them.

Get yourself a great marketing agency or make sure you have a marketing whiz on your team. The best branding in the world will go nowhere unless it is properly marketed, and whomever handles your marketing must understand what motivates people.

To be clear, when I work with clients, we take them through the entire P²P Process, including all of the business and strategy development outlined in this step. However, everything needs to be tailored to your specific business. So my attempting to do anything more than just outline the steps here in this book wouldn't be prudent.

Marketing plans are essentially problem/solution documents. You will find many marketing plan outlines. Our process is to start at the end (outcome/goals) and work backwards and includes the following steps:

1. Defined Outcome/Goals
2. Product Description
3. SWOT
4. Research
   a. Business Environment Analysis
   b. Market Research /Market Segmentation
5. Product Positioning/Marketing Mix
6. Budget
7. Execution
8. Evaluation

As an example, here is a synopsis of a detailed, 35-page plan we devised for one of our university clients. It is an adapted version of the outline we use, geared specifically for this client. Each of the categories was fleshed out to its maximum. As always, we worked with the client so everyone was crystal clear on each and every point, so we could create the best path for the product.

Example 16.2

University of XXXXX Marketing Plan Preliminary

Outcome/Goals (The Assignment)

> **What:**
>> Build perception and strengthen positioning of XXXXX School of Business Administration as a top-tier institution of higher learning—an elite business school of the caliber of Wharton.
>
> **Where:**
>> Internationally.
>>
>> (We went on to define 15 specific countries.)
>
> **Why:**
>> We are looking to attract qualified candidates and a talented faculty and engage alumni for support dollars.
>>
>> (We created a criterion for what constitutes a qualified candidate and talented faculty and a plan to attract them. Next, we created marketing strategies to attract alumni support.)

Description the University Today (Product Description)

> + Newly hired Dean XXXXXX brings a new vision to the school.
> + Global perspective
> + New and renowned talent
> + Multi-disciplinary streams
> + Innovative research and curriculum
> + Bilingual programs

3. Biggest Challenges

> General perceptions have not yet caught up to all the innovations and changes that have taken place.

(We did a complete SWOT Analysis: Strengths, Weaknesses, Opportunities and Threats.)

4. What are the Metrics for Success? (Research)

+ Improved ranking
+ Increase in applications (of higher caliber)
+ Improvement in student perceptions
+ Increase in PR mentions

(To determine the metrics, we performed market and segmented research)

5. Steps We Will Take to Create a Compelling Brand (Product Positioning/Marketing Mix)

(This is a good example of how branding and marketing intersect)

Step A: Create a compelling brand idea
Examining Four Areas
The University

The brand it is and the brand it wants to be.

The Competitive Framework

Determining opportunities to deposition the competition.

The Consumer

Key insights into the various student populations.

Cultural Context

Identifying major trends and counter trends that can be leveraged.

Step B: Validate the idea

Determine consumer and behavioral motivation.

Is it the right idea?

Is this the right time?

Are we in the right place?

At the right price?

Step C: Leverage the idea: connecting with the target

Use criteria for attracting qualified candidates to define the composite customer.

What are their motivations?

How will you reach them emotionally and financially?

How do they get their information delivered?

Take all of this information and build a Customer Connections Plan.

(We created a day-in-the-life of our target customer: he consumes most information electronically via the iPhone, iPad or similar devices, plus on the computer; he reads the print versions of Wall Street Journal and USA Today; consumes other news online via CNN, Yahoo! News and The Daily; avid watcher of ESPN both on the computer and on TV; dates via Match.com; has a HootSuite account etc.; is an online gamer; watches Comedy Central. We took this information and planned our advertising and marketing campaign around these and other targets).

Step D: Flawless execution

+ Project management
+ Status reports
+ Budget control reports
+ Estimating
+ Press checks
+ Extranet
+ FTP site
+ Weekly contact reports

Step 5: Evaluation/Metrics

+ Quarterly relationship check-in
+ Post-mortem on all communication programs
+ Review and refine metrics
+ Refine action plan

I know that having a professional marketing expert guide your business development makes the sailing smoother later. If you choose to go it alone, start with the resources I talk about in this section, get with your partner and begin building together. Know that because you now have a strong Human Foundation, the process will be much more fluid and easier to navigate.

17

CONCLUSION
WHAT I HAVE LEARNED IS THIS

Every failure brings with it the seed of an equivalent success.
—Napoleon Hill

I used to roll my eyes at those who prattled on about how they "learned so much" from their failures.

You know what? (she asks, eyes now sheepishly downward . . .)

It's true.

My partnership defeat gave me the opportunity to unveil who I really am and the steel of which I am made. I always knew I had strength. But strength of its own accord is never enough.

Through this experience, I met my self. You will too. I practically bled to death to finally see it. I guess that is my process (clearly I needed a new one). Please. I'm begging you. Take a different road.

By now you have likely realized that the magic of the Partnersh*t-to-Par+nership Process and the Human Foundation is not simply confined to the business partnership space. Think about how important knowing these things would be to your relationship, marriage, volunteer work, parenting and so on.

A partnership that works does so because the people involved understand that, like them, it's never "finished." A partnership is a living, breathing organism, subject to shifts as seismic as an earthquake and as seemingly insignificant as a sneeze. All need your full attention. That sneeze can turn into full-blown double pneumonia before you know it and deliver a fatal blow. Pay attention. Listen. Talk. It's all-important.

There is no doubt in my mind that throughout history, the human foundation has held up this world in the rockiest of times, even when those humans who don't subscribe to this philosophy have gone out of their way to destroy everything. What gets us through each and every disaster that ever happens? People. Joining together for a common cause. Sharing the dream in partnership with one another.

There's nothing more human than that.

+ + + + + + +

These documents are intended as examples only, and the content will not be the same for your partnership. Every partnership is different, and each agreement will reflect the personalities of and issues relevant to the partners. Because of the differences in partners and types of businesses, there is no real template that can apply to all. Additionally, each state has different laws, and each legal entity is managed differently.

However, please feel free to use these examples as a guidepost for your agreement, but be sure to make it your own. Your Partnership Plan is your road map that corresponds to the values, goals, accommodations and solutions you have established when you built your Human Foundation. Be sure to consult an attorney and financial planner to complete the Compensation section and to review the entire document for any legal red flags.

Because of the nature of this document, it will not be considered a legal document. Rather, it is a moral and ethical document, and carries all the weight and responsibilities thereof. Sign it and stand by it. We also recommend that all partners sign a separate Partnership Agreement or Operating Agreement drafted by your attorney.

Example A.1

[1]LISA STONE AND MARIANNE NESBITT
ABP PRINTING, LLC

This partnership between cousins Lisa and Marianne is an extension of a decades-old family-owned printing business that had grown obsolete and was in danger of going out of business. Rather than let tradition die, these women, both of whom at one time or another have worked in the business, decided to purchase and continue the business by embracing the new technologies that were once considered the enemy. They found a new way to compete.

Their Human Foundation Partnership Plan is reflective of their forward-thinking mindsets, nod to tradition and embrace of consciousness as the bedrock for how they will work together. They dug deep and used language that was important to them. While the language might seem feminine, Marianne is a dominant-masculine personality. It's important to understand that dominant masculines can still be as heart-based as the dominant feminines. Marianne's allusion to "battleground" and "soldiers" connotes her masculine approach to doing business, but she creates a

---

1 Partner and business names and information, and some financial details, have been changed to protect the privacy of our clients.

nice balance in her use of the word "heartfelt" when she describes what partnership means to her. Lisa, the money person, is extremely contribution-focused and has developed product ideas that she feels will serve the business and the world.

These two are a good match and have addressed issues that may cause friction. They are also aware and respectful of the stats on family-owned businesses and have seen their fathers as positive role models, and their fathers before that.

According to Stacy Perman from Bloomberg's Businessweek/Small Business, family- owned businesses continue to form the backbone of the American economy, accounting for 50% of U.S. gross domestic product, and some 35% of Fortune 500 companies are family-controlled. She adds that some of the world's largest corporations, from Wal-Mart (WMT) to News Corp. (NWS) to Ford Motor (F) are family businesses. But, she says, regardless of size, all family businesses face significant challenges of continuity, longevity, and ultimately success.

Harvard Business Review's George Salk and Henry Foley report that nearly 70% of family-owned businesses fail or are sold before the second generation gets a chance take over, and that only 10% remain active, privately held companies for the third generation to lead. "In contrast to publicly owned firms," they add, "in which the average CEO tenure is six years, many family businesses have the same leaders for 20 or 25 years, and these extended tenures can increase the difficulties of coping with shifts in technology, business models and consumer behavior."

Finally, they warn that family firms in developing markets face new threats from globalization. "In many ways," they say, "leading a family-owned business has never been harder."

Lisa and Marianne hope to debunk the adage that the 1st generation starts the business, the 2nd generation builds the business and the 3rd generation kills the business.

Our Human Foundation Partnership Plan:
This Partnership is About Us and How We Will Move Ahead Together, With Eyes on the Future, Yet Mindful of the Past

Name of Business:	ABP Printing, LLC
Date Established:	4/6/2011
Legal entity:	Limited Liability Corporation (LLC)
Address:	xxxxxxx
Our Vision:	"Once great; great once more."
Our Mission:	To be come the leading provider of printed and electronic goods and messaging via a patented technology that delivers stunning quality at an affordable cost.

Our Onliness Statement:

What:	The only printing company with a technology
How:	that will place us at the forefront of how printing is created and delivered
Who:	for customers
Where:	across the globe
Why:	who want their printing fast, stunningly beautiful and unbelievably well priced
When:	during a time when cost is the main determinant of purchasing.

Introduction:

This Human Foundation Partnership Plan is a joint creation of Lisa Stone and Marianne Nesbitt, with the help of our consultants and legal and financial advisors.

We have come together to resurrect a business that is meaningful to both of us. This business has been in our family for decades, and our fathers, who were the last owners, brought in outside partners that we feel were ultimately detrimental to the business. While we understand that changing technologies and price considerations were also responsible for the near-failure of this business, we believe that "What was once great can be great once more." All we need is a better mousetrap.

We have that. We believe this must become a family business once again, and we will be launching a printing technology that we believe will change how the industry works.

And now we want to change how a partnership works. Our goal in creating this document is to secure a strong foundation for our partnership and our business.

We intend that this document will do the following:

- Open and keep open the door to constant communication;
- Create a basis for how we relate and operate;
- Create trust between us;
- Clarify policies and processes;
- Explore and accommodate our unique personalities so that we each feel we can be our true selves in this enterprise;
- Use that exploration to define and manage areas of compatibility and conflict;
- Manage and mitigate any conflicting issues that we might have with each other;
- Define our wishes, dreams, values; fears; goals; and outcomes;

- Create a platform for conflict resolution;
- Develop dissolution and exit strategies.

We both understand the inherent dangers specific to family-owned businesses, and are making all efforts to maintain and nurture our lifelong love and respect for each other. We both agree that our relationship comes first, and we clearly understand the pitfalls that partnership can create for other relationships. We saw our fathers work respectfully and happily together for decades, and their fathers before that. It is our #1 commitment to follow this lead.

We have set forth 6 important and achievable goals for the next 12 months:

1. Register and secure the patent pending on Lisa's idea and begin prototype development with engineer;
2. Review all leases and restructure current workflow to cut operating costs by 25%;
3. Identify and secure a Board of Directors who can be instrumental in not just furthering our financial success but our community and industry standing as well;
4. Identify and secure at least 5 new revenue-heavy clients that result in $4 million in billings, based on our criteria scale;
5. $7m in annual billings for fiscal 2012, with an 8% net profit margin;
6. By Summer 2011, complete the company's new name, branding and positioning to reflect this new era.

The personal comments and promises in this plan are meant to document our exploration into developing our Human Foundation, and the resulting verbal commitments to each other and to the company. We understand that because of the nature of this document, it may be determined to not be legally binding. To accommodate this eventuality, we will also be signing a separate, legal document drafted by our attorney.

To us, this document is morally and ethically binding, which goes beyond the law of the land. Both documents together will solidify our unyielding commitment to create a solid, strong partnership and business that will stand even during trial and tribulation.

Lastly, this is a living document, which means we will review, adapt, shift, change or update it to reflect changing circumstances, roles or economic times.

Lisa Stone _____

Marianne Nesbitt _____

April 6, 2011

Partner #1 Information:
  Name: Lisa Stone
My Filter Is:
  Nurturing
What Partnership Means to Me:
  This Partnership is About Us. I stand here, next to my partner, in full integrity of vision, mission and outcome, to support, respect, trust, teach, learn and contribute not just to her and to me, but also to our customers, employees and vendors, and the community.
Job Title:
  CFO
Job Description:
  Define processes; implement structures; strategic planning to support projected annualized growth; manage administrative, financial and

program systems; active member of the senior management team.

Ownership:

40%

Partner #2 Information:

Name: Marianne Nesbitt

My Filter Is:

Action

What Partnership Means to Me:

This Partnership is About Us. Partners are more than just business associates; they are soldiers who go into battle together every day. Our battleground is business, and having a partner who can strengthen our business' position, ranks and strategies to create heartfelt, all-around success is something I have dreamed about. Now that dream is reality. I am that person for Lisa, for myself and for our company.

Job Title:

Director of Sales and Marketing

Job Description:

Responsible for creating and implementing strategic branding, sales and marketing plans that help to achieve annualized projected growth; new product development; co-management of the company with the CEO; provide leadership for all sales, marketing and PR efforts; oversee hiring and firing within department; oversee hiring and firing company-wide with HR and CEO; monitor budgets; active member of senior management team.

Percentage of Ownership:

60%

Here's What We Stand For:

Our core values have been established as the basis for decisions that we will make in both our partnership and our day-to-day business operations. We agree to revisit this document at least annually, but sooner if we find ourselves in unpleasant territory. We will not let sh*t get in the way of our dreams, goals and promises to each other.

Our Core Values:
Profitability
We are profitable in all relationships, not just in dollars, but in goodwill, health, contribution, community and spirituality.

Fairness
We stand for each other and all others so that everyone wins.

Sharing
The keyword for our partnership is Us. We know that our best will come from sharing both our victories and our defeats. We stand together to learn the lessons of each.

Innovation
Our family paved the way for excellence in this business for more than 60 years. We are honored to pick up the gauntlet and move ahead with courage, dignity and a respect for that tradition.

1. Characterization: Who We Are

Lisa:

I am family-oriented first and foremost. This includes a deep respect for both my family and this family business. Through our Human Foundation exploration, I was reminded that I am a wife and mother first and that I have never, and will not now, allow anything to intrude in or damage this part of my life.

I live to serve and help. And now, I have taken this step to add ownership of this family business to things that I love and care for. That's what's so wonderful about this for me: I feel like I can operate a successful business without feeling alienated from what is important to me. This business IS family and I will nurture it as I do my family at home. Some of these people worked for Dad for a decade or more, and that makes them family. However, I have been clear with Marianne that I will defer to my home family first. If something comes up at home, that has to be my priority.

I am very left-brained and love the order of numbers and how they make linear sense to me. I also love that my CFO duties are something I can do in the quiet and privacy of my home, if necessary, which I have done for years. My commitment is to create a financial scenario where ultimately this business will be brought back to profitability. We have many employees who count on us. We took over a troubled business, and I managed to avoid a bankruptcy filing, which would not have been to the company's advantage. So I know how to manage a dollar. I have told Marianne that the only ship I know how to run is a tight ship, so budgets will have to be bible. Because she's less detail-oriented than I am, we have agreed to analyze all expenditures for cost/payoff, and even though I am the minority partner, we have agreed that I will have veto power in this one area.

I do not want to be the big boss. Marianne is much better at that than I am. We have agreed to work together with our CEO on big decisions, but the day-to-day stuff goes to Marianne and the CEO.

I won't work weekends, and if the kids have evening events during the week, I won't be available to be onsite then either. To prevent any interruption of workflow, Marianne and I have both agreed to a regular schedule of deliverables from me. I also request ample notice for board or other administrative meetings.

I am fairly even-tempered and am happiest holed up with my spreadsheets and other financial documents. I'm also great with the employees but am awful when it comes to conflict. But I can definitely be counted on to attend events deemed important to furthering the business and am here to help Marianne with customers. I'm pretty good at that too.

I Promise To:

- Treat Marianne and our partnership with utmost respect;
- Cherish our team;
- Serve my family;
- Serve the company;
- Work a minimum of 55 hours/week and complete my work no matter where I am;
- Be available for all partnership conversations and meetings;
- Provide strategic financial planning and clear, weekly reporting;
- Make solid financial decisions for the company and exercise my veto power only when it will achieve a positive outcome;
- Defer to Marianne on management issues;
- Be sure to help Marianne slow down if she starts moving too fast;
- Maintain partnership confidentiality.

Marianne:

Batman Strikes! I get fired up by creativity, people and accomplishments and am as right-brained as they come. So Lisa already knows I have an inherent disrespect for budgets. Most of us creative types do. I'm fast-moving and tend not to think things through as well as she does. So we have agreed to let her be the Major Domo of budgets and give her yay or nay powers after we have reviewed the plusses and minuses together. And I will be Major Domo of the rest of the business. In the end, we both want a profitable business and we want to have fun doing this.

This business has been a big part of my life for most of my life, and I am happy to lead it into this century. Cousin Lisa and I share a great love for this place and I will do whatever I can to make it fly. I'm a hands-on, day-to-day fixture here and this is my priority. I'll cover for Lisa if her family calls. I trust her responsible nature.

I'm reactive (just ask my husband) and love Lisa's relative calm. I have been known to muscle my way around, even from the time I was a kid. Our dads worked together beautifully for a long time and I know we can too. I get really bugged when people miss deadlines. Mine is a deadline business. Marianne and I have agreed to schedule our business so she can run out if she has to and I will feel secure that her work is done. She has also come up with some awesome product ideas. My job will be to relationship those ideas to the proper JV partners so we can all do well. I'm excited!

I Promise To:

- Treat Lisa and our partnership with the utmost respect;
- Listen more!

- Bring my best creative brain to work every day;

- Respect the culture that is in place and be respectful about the changes I make;

- Respect the team;

- Respect Lisa's financial decisions;

- Co-manage operations with our CEO;

- Take a minute to think before I act;

- Respect Lisa's need to put family first;

- Nurture and develop Lisa's product from prototype to market;

- Maintain partnership confidentiality.

2. Collaboration: How We Will Work Together

Lisa:

Again, my family comes first but I am 100% in this with Marianne. I can work from home if that's what has to happen from time to time, without disturbing the office workflow. Because I am great at nerdy tasks like accounting, bookkeeping, budgeting, financial planning and so on, Marianne can expect top-notch planning and timely reporting from me, which is critical to running a business. I have years of experience doing this at this very company so I know what I'm doing. I expect Marianne to adhere to our plans and not attempt to overspend.

I am thrilled to have Marianne as my partner. She's talented, honest, dynamic and lots of fun. If she had declined, I would have sold. I did not want to do this alone.

I know I am not such a good manager. I don't like conflict and have a hard time hiring, reprimanding or firing people. Because many of our employees have been here a long time and aren't up to date on what we need to do to move this business forward, we understand that some will not survive this transition to new ownership. I cannot bring myself to fire any of these people. Marianne will work with Ted, our CEO, to do those things. She's a bit of a multitasker and I'm a little afraid she'll spread herself too thin. She assures me she will not and I have promised her I will let her know if she starts to race.

Marianne's husband has a tendency to get involved in our business and it irritates me. He owns part of this property and is entitled to his proceeds as a landlord, but he has no say in this business. While I love my cousin-in-law, I don't want him involved in our business or partnership, just as I don't get involved in his. He is an accountant too, and at times crosses the line with me. Marianne has assured me she has spoken to him and that he will not intrude. If he does, Marianne has given me permission to speak to him about this directly. She's a very strong and confident person and is secure enough to not let this become an issue between us. I know this because it's happened before and she has not taken sides. Rather, she's let us work it out ourselves.

Marianne and I have worked here together before, just not as partners. While I've been here all along, she has come back into the fold and is bringing in new clients, important creative blood and innovative thinking. I am committed to not having this partnership thing get between us. As owners and partners, we know the stressors will be different. So we have agreed to create a monthly "Communication Session" where we bring the list of irritations or complaints that we have had in the past month to the table to discuss and solve. We have agreed to open each session by reading our "What Partnership Means to Me" statements to get us centered and into a state of gratitude.

I Promise To:

- Be grateful every day that Marianne and I are partners;
- Be strong but firm should Marianne's husband become intrusive to the business;
- Write down any issues that are irritating me and resolve them with Marianne at the monthly Communication Session;
- Support Marianne's decisions about employee termination or new hires, especially in the art department. I reserve the right to weigh in on employee issues having to do with my department.

Marianne:

It's good to be back here at the company. I took a huge leap of faith to do this, giving up a great career and a big salary at my old company. Am I scared? You bet, but I am also excited. I want this. I am tired of working hard for someone else. I know the risks and have put up a lot of money to make this happen, but I'd rather make money for us than for someone else. Plus, it's good to be home again.

I don't want to do this alone. Lisa is the perfect person for me to partner with because she knows where all the dead bodies are buried. Also, she's a human calculator. I'm more like a human cash card, but am used to working within budget because I had to in my last position. Since this is my money on the line, I'll be sure to toe that line!

Lisa is also really relaxed, and I am not. I'm the one who's always hopping around from cool project to cool project. I like change and I like fast-moving days, and this business is filled with both. I also like a challenge. Turning a print business into something that can stand up in a digital world is a real challenge, but we're doing it. In addition to other great ideas that we have, I am convinced Lisa's product idea will be a game-changer. In fact, this, more than anything else, is what made me decide to buy into the company.

I am walking into this with approximately $3 million in new business, a result of the many amazing contacts I have amassed over the years. I also have decades of experience in marketing and sales. So I know how to position and sell us to a new audience. I work hard and keep late and often odd hours. But it's not a problem for me because the sale is there when it's there. I'm there to grab it. Lisa is cool with that too, since she has those demands of her own.

I admire Lisa for many things and trust her completely. She's chill and being with her is like taking a Xanax. (I mean that in a good way.) Right now I have no reservations about how we will work together but love the idea of the monthly "Communication Session" because I have been in this life long enough to know that things will come up.

And about my husband: I'll keep him out of this. He's a good guy and wants only the best for us.

I Promise To:

- Respect all budgets;
- Hire the best and brightest, with budget firmly in mind;
- Nurture my industry contacts for the betterment of the company;
- Grow this company to a global level over the next 10 years;
- Create a top-notch sales team;
- Understand that I am really a Producer first and operate in that

framework most of the time;

- Stay focused on those items that are high priority;

- Not micromanage;

- Not take too much on, as is my tendency. I will balance my duties and let Ted do his job as CEO. I'll be there to help him, not do his job.

3. Communication: How We Will Listen, Talk and Learn

Lisa:

I loved that we talked about email in our P^2P sessions. I use it all the time and prefer to communicate that way, but it has definitely gotten me into trouble since I'm a bit reserved and I'm told that sometimes I come off as unfriendly. So Marianne and I have promised to use email for nonemotional conversations only. For the real stuff, we will talk face-to-face.

I'm pretty quiet and like it when my office is quiet. I guess that makes sense; you need quiet to think analytically and work with numbers. Marianne is one exuberant lady, but we have the luxury of a big workspace. Her office is near the art department at the other end of the plant, so I don't hear her. She has promised to stop barging into my office. It's disruptive and often breaks my train of thought. I really dislike that. So now she'll shoot me an email or text asking if I am free, and of course I will do the same for her. I'd say I'm in a good mood most of the time. But look out if I get overtired. This is why I have said my family will come first if there's an emergency. If I stretch myself too thin I come unglued and it affects everything I do. I get cranky and that's not good.

I Promise To:

- Use email as a tool and not a weapon;

- Not allow myself to get tired or overstressed;

- Take a break if I am feeling overwhelmed;

- Go to the gym regularly.

Marianne:

I guess I am just a natural-born performer, because I love to get in front of people and talk, talk, talk. While this is great for sales, apparently Lisa doesn't always appreciate me. So we've agreed to text or email each other if we need to speak while she's working during the day. I'm okay with that, though I am not a huge fan of email. Some days I open my computer and there are 100 messages waiting for me. Thank God for my assistant.

I'm pretty out there in terms of mood—happy and excited more often than not. But do not make me angry. Lisa knows from as far back as when we were kids that I can get really ticked off if provoked. And what provokes me are laziness, missing deadlines, attitude and not caring. That makes me nuts and I respond by getting dead quiet. It scares people. It also takes me awhile to let go of things and I've been known to carry a grudge. I've promised Lisa to talk to her immediately (not wait for the Communication Session) if something is pushing me to my boiling point.

I Promise To:

- Stop barging into Lisa's office;

- Watch my tendency to get angry. If I am feeling like I'm going to boil, I promise to talk to Lisa no matter what.

4. Compensation: What We Want; What We Bring

Lisa:

It had reached the point where this company was going to close, and that thought broke my heart. I couldn't let it happen without trying to save it, so I approached Marianne to see if perhaps she might be interested in doing something here together. I had come up with at least one winning idea that I believed would not just save the business but change the industry. She loved it and I'm so happy she was at the time in her life where this was something she could get involved in. Plus, she's the one who can develop this idea and sell it.

I also had part ownership in the building that houses our business, an estate gift to me from my father. There were three other owners, and they either wanted to be bought out or they would vote to sell. That would be a 3-1 vote that I would lose. I did not have the assets to make this large a purchase, but Marianne did. So she stepped up and bought the remaining 60% ownership. So we, along with our husbands, own the property and lease it back to the business.

I wanted to be a partner but not be THE partner. I've always been a bench player and am great at it. My goals are to stay with this company for at least the next 15 years and then retire. We are creating an exit strategy that will work for both of us, renewable annually. While this is a long-standing business, in many respects we must treat it as a start-up. There is a huge gap between what was and what should be, but I am also very aware that we have many loyal employees who are scared right now. I will do my utmost to protect them, but realize some may not survive our growth.

We worked hard, and talked to our attorney and an outside financial planner (to avoid conflict of interest), to agree on who was bringing and doing what, and how we would be compensated.

I'm looking for security and continuation of tradition. I'm very profit-driven, which will be critical to the survival of this nearly failed business. I wanted a smaller ownership because I am comfortable with my position here and have been for years. There's not much I need in the way of creature comforts that I don't already have. My end goal is to leave my kids a legacy, both in dollars and tradition. I own part of the building and am happy owning part of the business. We agree that 50-50 is not how we want to work.

Marianne:

Not only was I thrilled to come back and help take over this business, but also I realized that the value of the real estate would be a hedge against a potential business failure. If for some reason we did not survive, I would have this valuable real estate to sell. That made my decision easier. My husband and I bought the remaining property shares together so he is my partner in any transactions having to do with real estate. He and I are paying the debt service on our RE loan and leasing the property back to the company, as are Lisa and her husband. We all act as landlords and neither spouse is involved in the company in any way. Additionally, I put up $600,000 to purchase the remaining shares of the company.

COMPENSATION DETAILS
COMPANY VALUATION

$1,000,000.00 (Liquidation value)

WHAT WE BRING	MARIANNE	LISA
A. CAPITAL CONTRIBUTION		
CASH	$400,000	$600,000
DELIVERY DATE FOR CONTRIBUTION	Over 5 years	Over 5 years
EQUIPMENT	Included in Valuation	Included in Valuation
INTELLECTUAL PROPERTY	TBD	0
TOTAL VALUE OF CAPITAL CONTRIBUTION	$400,000	$600,000
B. PROFIT/LOSS DISTRIBUTION- PROPORTIONAL		
% OWNERSHIP	40% of total	60% of total
C. PERSONAL EQUITY	New, game-changing product idea, patent pending	Marketing and Sales expert
	Honest, ethical, trustworthy,	$3M in new business
	25 years' experience at the company	Massive industry connections
	Rapport and a good reputation with employees, customers and vendors	Money
	CFO for 15 years	Vision for the Company
	Stable, part of the company's history and calming to those who fear the new ownership	Innovative thinker with connections to bring in fresh thinkers
	Highly committed to the company; long track record	Tremendous salesperson with documented success
		Has won industry awards and is well-known
		Family

Figure A.1 *Capital and other investments.*

MANAGEMENT

The Company will be co-managed by Marianne M. Nesbitt and the Company CEO, Lisa Stone, will have veto on budgetary items.

OPERATIONS

No partner in the Company shall be personally liable for the expenses, debts, obligations or liabilities of the Company, or for claims made against the Company.

Partners shall be reimbursed by the Company for organizational expenses paid by the partners. The Company shall be authorized to elect to deduct organizational expenses and start-up expenditures as permitted by applicable law.

Partner shall vote in proportion to their partnership interests in this Company, unless otherwise required by applicable law or by the Company's formation document filed with the State of Florida. A matter shall be approved if a majority of the partnership interests vote in favor of the matter.

Partners shall not be paid as partners of the Company for performing any duties associated with such partnership. Partners may be paid, however, for any services provided in any other capacity for the Company, whether as managers, officers, employees, independent contractors or otherwise.

The Company shall hold an annual partnership meeting at the time and place decided by management and communicated to all partner between 30 and 60 days before the regular meeting. In addition, any partner may call a special partnership meeting at any time by communicating to all other partner the plan to schedule a special meeting. Notification of partnership meetings may be in person, in writing, by telephone, by facsimile, or by any other form of electronic notice reasonably expected to be received by all partners. Special partnership meetings shall take place at the time and place stated in the meeting notification. Any business may be discussed and conducted at partnership meetings. Partnership meetings may be held without the attendance of all partners as long as partner holding a majority of partnership interests attend the meeting.

Written notice of the decisions or approvals made at all partnership meetings shall be mailed or delivered to each non-attending partner promptly after the meeting. Written minutes of the discussions and proposals at a partnership meeting, and the votes taken and matters approved at such meeting, shall be taken by one of the partner or a person designated at the meeting.

A copy of the minutes of the meeting shall be placed in the Company's record books after the meeting. Action required or permitted to be taken at an annual or special partnership meeting may be taken pursuant to written consent. Action by written consent may be taken without a meeting, without prior notice, and without a vote.

TAX AND FINANCIAL MATTERS

It is anticipated that at this time, this Company will not be treated as a corporation under federal income tax law. Instead, this Company will be treated for federal income tax purposes in the same manner as a partnership, unless there is only one, in which case the Company may choose to be disregarded as an entity for federal income tax purposes.

Within 75 days after the end of each tax year of the Company, a copy of the Company's state and federal income tax returns for the preceding tax year shall be mailed or otherwise provided to each partner in the Company, together with any additional information and forms necessary for each partner to complete their individual state and federal income tax returns.

The Company's management shall designate one or more banks or other institutions for the deposit of the funds of the Company, and shall establish such accounts as are reasonable and necessary for its business and investments.

Every year, the Company will distribute to the partners sufficient cash from the Company's profits to cover their projected income tax liability for their distributive share of items reported by the Company in Schedule K-1, unless all of the partnership interests vote against such distribution. All other distributions of the Company's profits will be made from time to time when and if approved by a majority of the partnership interests.

CAPITAL CONTRIBUTIONS

Partners shall make the initial capital contributions of cash, property or services approved by a unanimous vote of partner, on a delivery schedule approved by the partners.

The partners may agree from time to time by unanimous vote to require the payment of additional capital contributions by the partners by a mutually agreeable date.

No interest shall be paid on funds or property contributed as capital to this Company, or on funds reflected in the capital accounts of the partners.

A capital account shall be set up and maintained in the records book of the Company for each partner. The records book shall reflect each 's capital contribution to the Company, increased by each 's share of profits in the Company, decreased by each 's share of losses and expenses of the Company, and adjusted as required in accordance with applicable provisions of the Internal Revenue

Code and corresponding income tax regulations. No partner shall be given priority or preference with respect to other partner in obtaining a return of capital contributions, distributions or allocations of the income, gains, losses, deductions, credits or other items of the Company. The profits and losses of the Company, and all items of its income, gain, loss, deduction and credit, shall be allocated to partner according to their partnership interests.

Cash from the Company's business operations, as well as cash from a sale or other disposition of the Company's capital assets, may be distributed from time to time to the partner in accordance with their partnership interests, as may be decided by a majority of the partnership interests.

If the Company does not have sufficient cash to pay its obligations, either partner may agree to advance all or part of the needed funds as a loan to the Company on terms acceptable to the Company's management. Any such advance shall be treated as a loan to the Company and shall not constitute an additional capital contribution.

NEW PARTNERS AND STOCK TRANSFER

No person may be admitted as an additional partner unless the admission is approved by a majority of the partnership interests and the additional partnership interest is purchased by such person for fair consideration.

Partners may not transfer their partnership interests in the Company unless all of the partnership interests approve the admission of the transferee into this Company. Further, partners may not encumber a part or all of their partnership interests in the Company by mortgage, pledge, security interest, lien or otherwise, unless the encumbrance has first been approved in writing by the Company's management, which approval may not be unreasonably withheld.

Notwithstanding the above provisions, partners may assign an economic interest in their partnership interests to any another person without the approval of the other partner or managers. Such an assignment shall not include a transfer of voting or management rights in this Company, and the assignee shall not become a partner of the Company.

DISSOLUTION

Unless otherwise provided by applicable law or by the Company's formation document filed with the state of Florida, this Company shall be dissolved upon the first to occur of any of the following events: (a) written agreement of a majority of partnership interests to dissolve the Company or (b) entry of an order of dissolution by a court with jurisdiction over the Company.

- A partner who moves to dissolve must serve 6-month notice to other partner(s),

- If a partner chooses to dissolve the partnership, a 100% vote is required.

- If any partner leaves, the partnership will not automatically dissolve.

- Partnership Asset Distribution will be based on P/L Ratios.

- Both partners will offer their shares for sale to each other first, at a price agreed upon based upon a professional valuation by an uninvolved third party.

- Selling partner may offer shares for sale to someone outside the Company only if other partner declines to purchase them.

- Majority partner agrees not to sell the Company to any buyer for 10 years without the consent of minority partner. After 10 years, majority partner may sell her shares without consent.

- Attorney will establish a shares buyback program within 6 months of this signed agreement.

- Partners agree that should a great selling opportunity arise that would be in the best interests of both partners, that would be discussed separate from this agreement. After dissolution of the Company, its management shall diligently wind up and liquidate the business and affairs of the Company. The Company shall pay for all expenses of liquidation.

GENERAL

The Company's management may appoint officers, who shall have the responsibilities generally accorded to their positions, subject to the right of management to modify the responsibilities of such positions. Persons who fill these positions need not be partners or managers of the Company. The officers may be compensated or uncompensated according to the nature and extent of the services provided by such officers.

The Company shall keep at its principal business address a copy of all proceedings of partnership meetings, as well as books of account of the Company's financial transactions.

A list of the names and addresses of the current partnership of the Company also shall be maintained at this address, with notations on all transfers of economic interests to nonpartners and transfers of partnership interests to persons admitted into partnership in the Company. A list of the name and address of the Company's management staff shall also be kept at this address.

Copies of the Company's formation document filed with the state of Florida, a signed copy of this Agreement, and the Company's tax returns for the preceding three tax years shall be kept at the principal business address of the Company. Any partner or manager may inspect any and all records maintained by the Company upon reasonable notice to the Company. Copying of the Company's records by partners and managers is allowed, but reasonable copying costs shall be paid for by the requesting partner or manager.

The partners, managers and officers of this Company are authorized to perform all acts necessary to perfect the organization of this Company and to carry out its business operations expeditiously and efficiently. The Company's management may certify to other businesses, financial institutions and individuals as to the authority of one or more partners, managers or officers of this Company to transact specific items of business on behalf of the Company.

WHAT WE WANT	
LISA	MARIANNE
Salary of $175-200k	Salary of $275k
Company car as can be afforded	Company car as can be afforded
Monthly expenses to be determined by accountant	Monthly expenses to be determined by accountant
$2m term life insurance policy naming Marianne as beneficiary	$2m term life insurance policy naming Lisa as beneficiary
Disability policy that pays up to 80% of annual salary if I become incapacitated.	Disability policy that pays up to 80% of annual salary if I become incapacitated.
Gym partnership to be paid by the company	Support for and autonomy in my position
Flex time	Company adherence to our vision
Autonomy in the finance realm	Ability to hire and grow staff commensurate with company's growth
At least a PPO-level Medical coverage, based on cost	At least a PPO-level Medical coverage, based on cost
Balance in my life	Right of first refusal to buy Lisa out at time of her exit
Stable, part of the company's history and calming to those who fear the new ownership	
4 weeks for family vacation time, spread out over year	
Be bought out in 15 years	

Figure A.2   *Partner requirements.*

5. Contribution: What We Give; How We Serve

Lisa:

I am big on community involvement. ABP has always been a community player. Over the years we have sponsored local sports, education and medical charities. I wish to continue in this vein and Marianne agrees. Budget permitting, we will apportion a percentage of our income to charity. We have agreed that together we will pick the 501(c)(3)s that resonate with us.

I Promise To:

- Continue with my efforts to be philanthropic;
- Look for philanthropic opportunities that offer the greatest benefit based on our predetermined criteria;
- Make sure to align our philanthropy in a manner that is advantageous tax-wise, whenever possible.

Marianne:

Lisa and I are in total agreement on this one. In my last job, we had an intern program that brought us new talent all the time. We had a high intern hire rate. We're sitting in the middle of a virtual melting pot of multilingual creative talent. I will to work closely with the surrounding schools' art departments to nurture that talent.

I Promise To:

- Mine the creative community for the best possible talent;
- Develop a paid internship program around a set of criteria that will help the company and serve the intern's growth in their field.

6. Construction: What We Will Build

Lisa:

We both know taking on this business comes with risk, but I feel this in my heart. We're not just in the printing business; we're in the business of delivering creative visions affordably, to the world via print and electronic means. I think I have a Guttenberg soul; the printed page is in my blood. I know that no matter what innovations come along, there will always be a place for high quality, tactile, beautifully typeset products.

This business has fulfilled me for nearly two decades. Now, with Marianne's help and vision, I feel a renewed excitement and know we're on the way to leading a printing revolution that will change the industry.

We have agreed that our 5 most important goals for next year are:

1. Register and secure the patent pending on Lisa's idea and begin prototype development with engineer;

2. Review all leases and restructure current workflow to cut operating costs by 25%;

3. Identify and secure a Board of Directors who can be instrumental in not just furthering our financial success but our community and industry standing as well;

4. Identify and secure at least 5 new revenue-heavy clients that result in $4 million in billings, based on our criteria scale;

5. $7m in annual billings for fiscal 2012, with an 8% net profit margin

6. By Summer 2011, complete the company's new name, branding and positioning to reflect this new era

I Promise To:

- Make goal achievement job #1.

Marianne:

I am here because I see an opportunity to revolutionize the printing business. With my marketing and sales ability and Lisa's game-changing idea, I believe that we will not just turn this company around but step to the forefront of the industry. So yes, this business feeds my passion. Worst-case scenario would be a business failure. But like I said before, the risk is mitigated by the value of the real estate. Additionally, the liquidation value of the machinery and other assets would further soften the blow. So we're actually in a great position.

I Promise To:

- Make goal achievement job #1;
- Introduce an excited and innovative spirit not seen behind these walls in a long time.

7: Creation: How We Will Interact With the World

Lisa:

We have stepped up and created a plan that will serve as the foundation of our partnership and company. Designing the business is an exciting step and is based on real, actionable goes discussed in the last section.

I Promise To:

- Cherish and respect this partnership, business and opportunity.
- Be grateful each and every day.

Marianne:

This last section is my baby. I understand the value of the new approach to building a business, and we are working with the Business Model Canvas to strategize and execute our 5 most important goals. Additionally, the marketing department is already on the case, and based on our vision, mission and onliness statement, will have comps for us to review together by mid-May 2011.

I Promise To:

- Create a new brand that will cause a stir in the industry;
- Create a new business culture that will stress innovation and creativity;
- Co-create, with my partner, a new business model that will bring service, prosperity and fun back into a business we both cherish;
- Pace ourselves to grow a smart business, not a big business.

Let's Do This!!!!

Example A.2

[2]KEVIN MENENDEZ AND KARL WHITE

You met life/business partners Kevin and Karl back in Chapter 7. They are a different breed, and the long-format Partnership Plan just did not compute for them. Because both are visually oriented, too many words on paper make their eyes gloss over. So they created their own version of the Partnership Plan. In it, they honed in on the behaviors that were causing trouble, made their compromises, and then declared themselves in a powerful way. Remember that they have been together for a decade, so the ownership split, financials and other business strategies are already represented in a legal document drawn up by their attorney.

In a few short words, represented graphically, they incorporated everything they learned and all that they promised to themselves and each other. They determined that their core values are Respect, Health, Clarity, Accountability, Profitable, Beauty, Quality, Balance and Respect. They also determined that they would run their business by building a Foundation, Systems, Process and Solutions, and by creating Action and Results.

They were able to incorporate their compatibilities, conflicts and compromises into a core values format.

---

2   Partner and business names and information, and some financial details, have been changed to protect the privacy of our clients.

Our Human Foundation Partnership Plan:
Living Lives Through the Lens of Beauty

Name of Business:	Menendez Photography, Inc.
Date Established:	2004
Legal entity:	Sub-Chapter S Corporation
Our Vision:	Through beauty and indelible imagery, we will fuel creativity and empower people to be the best expressions of themselves.
Our Mission:	Offer powerful creative services and innovative visuals to a fashion-forward clientele by combining fashion and beauty photography with the latest technology.

Our Onliness Statement:

What:	The only high-fashion creative and photography house in the region
How:	that delivers stunning, innovative imagery in all manner of delivery systems
Who:	to a glamorous, fashion-forward clientele
Where:	in fashion centers throughout the world
Why:	who want transformative, glamorous imagery
When:	that will forever transcend time.

Partner #1 Information:

Name: Kevin Menendez

My Filter Is: Nurturing

What Partnership Means to Me:

Partnership means clarity, communication, listening, acknowledging, growing, learning and appreciating someone else's input and effort that make your job and life more complete. It means allowing oneself to discover common ground with another person so that together you achieve greatness.

Job Title:

Owner, Chief Creative Officer

Job Description:

Creative director, photographer, drive new business, networking, design and layout, photo retouching, work with production teams.

Ownership:

50%

Partner #2 Information:

Name: Karl White

My Filter Is: Security

What Partnership Means to Me:

Partnership is the ability to share thoughts and ideas without compromise, with someone who respects a different point of view than theirs. It's the ability to share this with a person who understands that theirs may not be the only way to do something.

Job Title:

Owner and Chief Administrative Officer

Job Description:

Create and manage office systems; manage bookings, billings, interact with accountant.

Ownership:

50%

HERE'S WHAT WE STAND FOR:

RESPECT

- Respect is the foundation for everything in our lives.
- We insist on respect for each other, others, our home, ideas, opinions, strengths and weaknesses.
- We will only work with people who have integrity.
- Kevin will stop interrupting and instead, listen.
- Kevin will be on time.
- Karl learned to speak up.
- Karl will not shut down; instead will discuss what's bothering him.
- Kevin will have respect for their home that doubles as their workspace. When working, he will not allow anyone to violate the off-limits areas of the space.
- Kevin will stop treating Karl like a child.

HEALTH

- We will change our eating habits to something healthier.
- The gym is a priority.
- We will only be in environments or around people who give off positive energy.
- God is in our lives.
- Kevin will continue with his AA meetings and be supportive of others in the program.
- Kevin will be supportive of Karl's need for privacy.

CLARITY

- Kevin works daily on staying focused.
- We will use process to become clear.

- We will both ask if we don't know something. No guessing or assuming.

PROCESS
- In business, we will follow the process.
- We will define processes together, with Karl in the lead.
- Karl will manage all processes.

SYSTEMS
- Karl needs systems to thrive; office, computer, day-to-day etc.
- Karl will develop all systems, and day-to-day decisions are his.
- Kevin promises to adhere to the systems.

ACCOUNTABILITY
- We are each accountable for our words, actions, deeds and solutions.
- Blame is not allowed ever, for any reason.
- We will be accountable for any results we deliver.
- Karl runs operations and will be accountable for their success or failure.
- Kevin will respect the process.

PROFITABLE
- Each of us has established boundaries in the business.
- No job started without a signed invoice.
- No jobs delivered without a deposit.
- We will be profitable in all relationships; profit is not just money but also goodwill, service, love, helping and friendship.
- Kevin will drive business; Karl will run the business.
- Karl needs to be secure financially.

- We will invest a percentage of our profits for future financial growth and retirement.

BEAUTY

- Beauty is a driving force in our business, environment and life.
- We are grateful for our lives and everyone in them.
- Beauty is love.

SOLUTION

- We will solve problems rather than dwell on them.
- Action is the way.
- We will not partake in passive aggressive behavior.

QUALITY

- No matter what we do, the result is quality.
- We insist on quality in everything that comes our way: love, relationships, food, sleep, rest, work, friends, activities.

BALANCE

- Kevin will work on tempering his workaholic ways.
- Karl will plan fun events and Kevin will keep his promise to attend.
- The dog rules.

Next, they brought their declarations to life. This text graphic is their version of a Partnership Plan. It hangs on their wall as a daily reminder, not just to each other, but also to everyone working with them, that this is what they stand for. Short, sweet, clear, concise and very inspiring.

CORE VALUES

1 The foundation of all we do is respect
for us, others, home, space, ideas, opinions, strengths, weaknesses

2 We maintain health
in our environment, spirit, body, mind

3 Clarity in all situations

4 Follow the process

5 Adhere precisely to systems
sales, management, operations, customer service, experiential

6 Accountability
for responsabilities, your actions and the solution

7 We are profitable
in all our relationships

8 Beauty is present

9 The solution is the action
not the result

10 Quality is the end result
of all our endeavors

11 We encourage balance
in our lifestyles. not all work. must play

Figure A.3 *Kevin and Karl's core values-based Partnership Plan.*

Kevin Menendez_____

Karl White _____

March 22 2010

APPENDIX B

BOOKS, BOOKS AND MORE BOOKS

I love books. The way they feel, smell, the cover art, the inspiring words, the laughs and tears, the lessons taught. The great books don't always teach only the lesson the writer intended; readers will take from them what they need. For various and not always obviously related reasons, I love and recommend the following:

Business Model Generation: A Handbook for Visionaries, Game Changers and Challengers by Alexander Osterwalder and Yves Pigneur

Designing Brand Identity: An Essential Guide for the Whole Branding Team by Alina Wheeler

Keys To The Vault: Lessons From the Pros on Raising Money and Igniting Your Business by Keith J. Cunningham

Working Together: Why Great Partnerships Succeed by Michael Eisner

Forming a Partnership and Making It Work: Entrepreneur Magazine's Legal Guide by Ira Nottonson

The Culture Code: An Ingenious Way to Understand Why People Around the World Live and Buy As They Do by Clotaire Rapaille

Beyond Disruption: Changing the Rules in the Marketplace by Jean-Marie Dru

Herd: How to Change Mass Behaviour by Harnessing our True Nature by Mark Earls

Purple Cow by Seth Godin

Zag: The #1 Strategy of High-Performance Brands by Marty Neumeier

That Used to Be Us: How America Fell Behind in the World It Invented and How We Can Come Back by Thomas Friedman

Tactical Transparency: How Leaders Can Leverage Social Media to Maximize Value and Build their Brand by Shel Holmes, John C. Havens and Lynne D. Johnson

Conscious Business: How to Build Value Through Values by Fred Kofman

Man's Search for Meaning by Viktor Frankl

Dying to Be Me by Anita Moorjani

Truman by David McCullough

The Fountainhead by Ayn Rand

The Next 100 Years: A Forecast for the 21st Century by George Friedman

And because I love to laugh...

Letters from A Nut by Ted. L. Nancy

APPENDIX C

You've heard me say this before: I am not a psychologist, MBA, financial planner or attorney. I am you. An everyday person who took on a partner, opened a business and hit the rocks.

This book has been about *my* experience and is from my perspective. Because the student was ready, these questions and this process literally downloaded from somewhere out there in my universe, and are a rich amalgam of all my years, personal experiences, filters and outcomes.

You have yours. In this time of microsecond communication, we have an advantage: we can instantly reach out and help each other. So, I am asking you: reach out and help.

I want to hear about your partnership experience. I want to know what questions you think need to be asked that I have not included, and why they are important to you. My greatest joy would be to create a movement among people who value humanity first; who understand the proper order of business architecture; and who are 100 percent committed to being excellent human beings.

I would call that movement A Human Foundation. Catchy, huh?

I will incorporate your input into the next edition, complete with full attribution. So names, please. You deserve credit for expressing your thoughts and wisdom. Stand up and be recognized! Go online at http://ahumanfoundation.com/contact and send me your thoughts and tell me about your process. Your experience. Your partnersh*t. Your way out.

＋ ＋ ＋ ＋ ＋ ＋ ＋

Thank you for reading. Thank you for your time. Thank you for your trust. I am grateful beyond words.

In fact, I am now, finally, speechless.

Until next time...

ABOUT THE AUTHORS
PATTY SOFFER

Patty Soffer is a renowned brand strategist and partnership coach who incorporates Building a Human Foundation into all that she does. Her path has taken her from a delightful childhood in a tiny midwestern town to a 15-year career as a top fashion, beauty and television model in New York, Milan and Tokyo. She opened a successful high-end fashion retail store, where, she says, her best decision was to hire a talented manager so she could pursue what she really loved to do, which was to learn and write. She went on to graduate magna cum laude at age 40, with a degree in journalism and mass communications.

Shortly thereafter, Soffer co-created one of the South's hottest branding and design firms with her business partner, all while raising her two kids as a single parent. Until its dramatic implosion, the firm stood front and center as an award-winning, rising star in the nation, serving a roster of clients that included McDonalds, Marriott, Heineken, Sol Melia Hotel Group, The Related Group, Turnberry Associates, Aventura Mall, Buccini Pollin Group, Perry Ellis, Dawson Company Atlanta, MDM Group's Metropolitan Miami, Midtown Miami, Gary Hall, Jr. Foundation for Diabetes, The Humane Society and many others. Over the years, the firm collected nearly 100 Addy and other industry awards and was named one of the *Hot 500* companies in the nation by Entrepreneur Magazine.

Currently, Soffer is consulting with businesses and partners who understand the value of building a Human Foundation, and also acts as a brand strategist for special projects. This is her third book.

VICKI ST. GEORGE

Victoria (Vicki) St. George, partner in Just Write Literary and Editorial Services, LLC, works with several literary agents to develop their clients' proposals and ghostwrite bestselling nonfiction books on wide-ranging subjects.

Over the past decade and a half, Vicki and her business partner, Karen Risch, have written and edited books published by Random House, HarperCollins, Simon & Schuster, Hay House, Thomas Nelson and John Wiley & Sons. They also have assisted and coached many authors who choose to self-publish through the daunting process of getting their books into print and into readers' hands.

Vicki combines her background in marketing with expertise in the different phases of book production and promotion, and extensive experience in all forms of collaborative writing and editing. Vicki, Karen and Just Write are proud to be known as the "successful authors' best-kept secret."